NEW YORK STATE ENGLISH LANGUAGE ARTS COACH, GRADE 8

BY STUART MARGULIES, PH.D. & MARIA GOUDISS

EDUCATIONAL DESIGN   EDI 808

ACKNOWLEDGMENTS

The authors wish to acknowledge:

Dickinson, Emily, "The Morns Are Meeker," from The Complete Works of Emily Dickinson.

Excerpt from "A Village Singer," by Mary E. Wilkins Freeman, from *A New England Nun and Other Stories*, 1891.

Excerpt from *Anna Christie*, by Eugene O'Neil, Horace Liveright Inc.

Excerpt from *Anne's House of Dreams*, by L.M. Montgomery, Grosset and Dunlap, NY.

Excerpt from "Boys of Other Countries," by Bayard Taylor, American Book Company.

Excerpt from "Immigration Experience," *The Virginia SOL History & Social Science Coach Grade 8*, by Vivienne Hodges, Educational Design, Inc., 1998.

Excerpt from *Of Human Bondage*, by W. Somerset Maugham, Doubleday and Co.

Excerpt from "Text Of Remarks At Wellesley College Commencement," by Barbara Bush, June 1, 1990. Online. Gifts of Speech. Available: http://gos.sbc.edu/a/allen.html. 16 July 1998.

Excerpt adaptation of "The Echo," by Elise Jane Jacobs, from *A Half-Century of Song, An Anthology of Hunter College Verse*.

Excerpt from "The Necklace," by Guy DeMaupassant, from *The Odd Number*, Harper and Brothers, 1889.

Horton, George Moses, "Liberty and Slavery," *The Hope of Liberty: Containing a Number of Poetical Pieces*, J. Gales & Son, Raleigh, NC.

TABLE OF CONTENTS

To the Teacher 5
To the Student 7

PART 1: READING 9
1 Recalling Stated Information 10
  Using Graphic Organizers to Recall
  Details 11
  Sequence 12
  Using Graphic Organizers to
  Determine Sequence 14
**2 Making Inferences and Drawing
  Conclusions** 21
  Cause and Effect 22
  Predicting Outcomes 24
**3 Using Context to Understand
  Vocabulary** 28
  Using Context Clues 28
  Phrases and Expressions 30
**4 Determining the Main Idea and
  the Details That Support It** 34
  Theme 36
  Supporting Details 37
  Using Graphic Organizers to
  Determine Main Ideas and
  Supporting Details 37
5 Analyzing Story Plots 43
  Problems and Resolutions 43
6 Analyzing Characters 48
  How Characters Change 50
  Using Graphic Organizers to
  Analyze Characters 51
7 Comparing and Contrasting 56
  Using Graphic Organizers to
  Compare and Contrast 56
  Comparing Characters 59
  Comparing Settings 60
  Interpreting and Comparing Maps 60
**8 Identifying the Author's
  Viewpoint and Purpose** 65
  Author's Viewpoint 65
  Purpose 66
  Using Graphic Organizers to
  Determine the Author's Viewpoint 68
  Persuasive Devices 69

**9 Understanding Figurative
  (Nonliteral) Language** 75

PART 2: WRITING AND LISTENING 81
10 Writing 82
  Punctuation 82
    End Marks 82
    Commas 83
    Apostrophes 84
    Capitalization 85
  Usage 86
  Spelling 88
11 Writing Strategies 91
  Using Details from the Passage 91
  Stay on Target 92
  Answering All Parts of the Question ... 93
12 Applying Your Writing Skills 97
  Writing Short and Long
  Responses 97
  Writing Answers Analyzing
  Character 102
  Writing Answers Comparing
  Characters 102
  Writing Answers Based on Two
  Selections 103
  Writing Answers Based on the
  Author's Purpose 107
  Writing Answers Based on Your
  Knowledge or Experience 108
13 Listening 112
  Note Taking 114

PART 3: PRACTICE TEST 129
Test-Taking Tips 130
Session 1 Multiple Choice,
                Listening/Writing 131
Session 2 Reading/Writing 149

TO THE TEACHER

This book is aimed at the development of higher-order reading competencies in eighth-grade students. It prepares students for the **New York State English Language Arts Test**. The test assesses students' comprehension strategies as well as their ability to synthesize information from a variety of sources.

Students are required in the test to read and analyze a wide range of genres, to demonstrate comprehensive proficiency in listening, and to prepare short and long written answers to many types of questions. The test employs three answer modes: multiple choice, short answer, and extended response. *The New York State English Language Arts Test Coach* covers each of these formats.

The selections teaching listening must be read to the student by the teacher. The selections are read twice. The student takes notes on the second reading. The student is not allowed to see the selections. All listening selections are found in the Teacher's Guide.

Selections on the **NYS English Language Arts Test** range from simple to difficult. Some questions assess the literal or recall level of reading performance, but most questions require higher-order reading skills. *The Coach* develops the full spectrum of reading levels, but most attention is directed to higher level skills.

Selections included in this book match **NYS English Language Arts Test** item profiles. They have been chosen for their high interest level.

Students benefit most when they can read the stories at a relaxed pace and have plenty of time for classroom discussion.

We hope and expect that students will enhance their reading and listening competencies and do better on the test. In the process, we hope that they will also enjoy the reading selections.

TO THE STUDENT

This book will help you become a better reader, listener, and writer. It will also help you do well on the **New York State English Language Arts Test** by showing you how to answer the types of exercises you will encounter on this test. Some of these may be different from anything you have seen before.

At the end of the book is a Practice Test which is like the **New York State English Language Arts Test**. You will find that it has some challenging exercises.

PART 1: READING

1. RECALLING STATED INFORMATION

On the **New York State English Language Arts Test**, you will sometimes be asked if you can remember a specific fact about a selection you have read. You might be asked:

* Who is the new captain?

* How much does the ticket cost?

* When will we be able to leave?

* How far did the home run go?

The best way to answer questions like these is, if you don't remember the answer, to check back through the selection.

Read Example 1. Then read the question which follows the passage. Before you answer the question, check back to make sure you have the correct answer.

Example 1

Who is the best-known person who lived in the Old West? Some people would say it's Buffalo Bill, the famous frontier scout and showman. Some would say it's a U.S. Marshall, Wyatt Earp. Some would say it is the great leader of the Native Americans, Chief Joseph.

But I think the most famous person from the Old West was Annie Oakley. Annie was the best rifle shot who ever lived. She almost never missed. Many men challenged her to contests of speed and accuracy. She won them all.

There are still many others who were very well known including the outlaws Jesse James and Billy the Kid. The Old West was full of colorful characters.

1   **The author thinks that the best-known person in the Old West was**

   A   Annie Oakley

   B   Buffalo Bill

   C   Chief Joseph

   D   Jesse James

The correct choice is **A**, Annie Oakley. If you checked back in the text you would find that the author thinks Annie Oakley was the most famous person in the Old West.

When you are answering a question about the details in a passage, you don't have to reread the entire selection. Skim through the selection until you find the facts you need.

USING GRAPHIC ORGANIZERS TO RECALL DETAILS

Example 2

Slavery in America began in the 1600's. Most slave labor was on Southern plantations which grew tobacco, cotton, and other crops. Besides picking the cotton used in America's export business, slaves helped in the building of railroads, canals, and roads. Many Americans hated slavery and wanted to end it. The United States was founded on a love of liberty, and slavery is the worst kind of tyranny. Yet soaring profits among slaveowners served to maintain the South as a bastion of slavery.

Slaveowners had field slaves and house slaves. Those slaves who worked in the fields of the plantation lived in crude log cabins. These crowded slave dwellings were devoid of normal "creature comforts." Wind and rain blew freely through the walls. The slaves had neither furniture, beds, nor privacy in these one-room shacks. A house slave lived in the home of the slavemaster. They lived in more comfort but worked very long hours. Whether house or field slave, none had the right to marry or to own property. And all were subject to brutal discipline.

Slaves often tried to escape. Some were successful but most efforts failed because of the difficulty of the task and the powerful network of the owners.

Slavery in the South ended on January 1, 1863 when President Lincoln issued the Emancipation Proclamation and finally in 1865, the 13th Amendment to the Constitution ended slavery throughout all of America.

—*From A Slave's View by Anna Millensen, Witchtree Publications.*

2 What fact is true of both a house and a field slave?

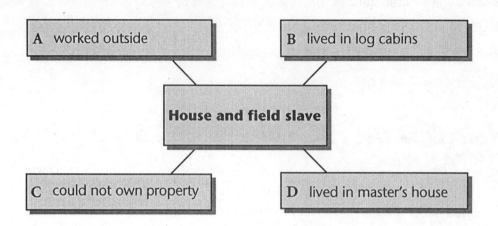

A worked outside	B lived in log cabins

House and field slave

C could not own property	D lived in master's house

If you check back in the passage, you will find that Choice **C** is correct.

SEQUENCE

The **New York State English Language Arts Test** sometimes asks you questions about what happened first or last. Key words like "before" and "after," or "first" and "last," help you to understand the order in which something happens. Read the next example and answer the question.

Example 3

At first Hillary felt nervous about the interview. She was worried about how she looked and what she should say. Then, when she arrived at the office where the interview was and saw the friendly atmosphere, she started to relax.

Finally, after it was over, she felt exhilarated. She was convinced she'd be hired.

3 What happened last?

A Hillary was nervous.

B Hillary was sure she'd get the job.

C Hillary worried about how she looked.

D Hillary arrived at the location of the interview.

Your teacher will discuss your answer.

Some passages have a clear sequence of events, even though they do not use common key words like "first" and "last." In cases like these, you may have to work out the sequence by reading the material carefully and looking for clues.

Some possible clues are the time of day, calendar dates, or ages.

Read Example 4 and decide the correct order of events.

Example 4

> She was only up for a few minutes when Tashena knew that something was wrong. Her head was aching and she felt tingly all over. She thought she might feel better if she went out for breakfast, but she felt worse walking in the cold air. Her knees felt wobbly, and it was hard for her to concentrate. Once she was in the coffee shop, she realized she wasn't hungry anymore. Nothing looked good to her. When the waiter asked her what she would like, she just sat there. She couldn't utter a word.

4   **Which came first?**

   A   Tashena couldn't utter a word.

   B   Tashena's knees felt wobbly.

   C   Tashena went inside the coffee shop.

   D   Tashena realized she wasn't hungry anymore.

The correct answer is **B**, Tashena's knees felt wobbly.

USING GRAPHIC ORGANIZERS TO DETERMINE SEQUENCE

Read this passage and then see how the parts of the story fit into a graphic organizer.

> The Cain family all love soccer. Paula learned first, joining the team less than a year after the family moved to Kansas. By the time Andy joined, the twins Alex and Peter, were already stars. Within a year, Andy was a super-star. All the family played well, but no one could compete with Andy.
>
> This month, he received two offers to play professionally.

Each box contains an event. These events are arranged in the order in which they occurred, with the earliest event at the left and the latest event on the right.

This graphic organizer shows the sequence of events.

The next example also deals with sequence. Read the passage and then look at the graphic organizer. It contains five boxes; one of them is empty.

Decide which event belongs inside the empty box.

Example 5

> Heat oven to 375 degrees. Fry the eggplant in hot oil after slicing and peeling it. Then layer the slices in a small casserole. Prepare the cheese sauce according to the directions. Pour over eggplant, dot with butter, and bake 45 minutes until golden brown on top. Let cool before serving.

5   **Which words belong in the empty box?**

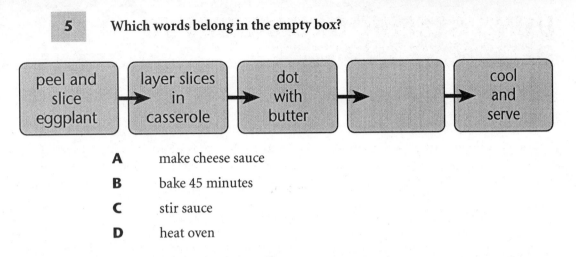

    A   make cheese sauce

    B   bake 45 minutes

    C   stir sauce

    D   heat oven

These instructions have five steps. The missing step was Choice **B**, "Bake 45 minutes." This belongs in the empty box. Here is the completed graphic:

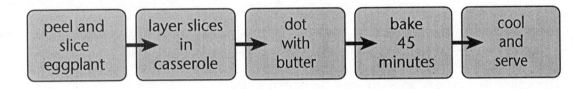

STRATEGIES AND TIPS
FOR RECALLING DETAILS AND
DETERMINING SEQUENCE

1. Read the selection. Then read the question. Look back in the selection for the answer.

2. You don't have to reread the entire selection to find the answer.

3. To determine sequence, look for key words, such as before and after, or first and last, to help you to understand the order in which things happened.

4. Look for clues, such as the time of day or the season, to help you figure out when things happened.

5. Read the selection carefully and try to figure out the order that makes the most sense for things to happen.

Read each of the selections below. Look carefully for the facts you need. Study the sequence. Check to make sure before you choose your answer.

SELECTIONS FOR PRACTICE

Selection 1

Babe Ruth was the greatest baseball player in history. He is still one of the most famous athletes who ever lived. As a youngster, Ruth was in trouble a lot. His parents sent him to St. Mary's School, a school that taught youngsters with problems. He played baseball there, and the priests were so impressed that they suggested he try out for the Major Leagues.

At first Ruth was a pitcher. In one World Series, he pitched 29 innings without letting the opposing team score even one run! But he was even more famous as a hitter.

The highest accomplishment for a hitter is to hit a home run. Some baseball players hit only one or two home runs in their entire career. Ruth hit 54 home runs in 1920, an unbelievable figure. Then he broke his own record in 1921, and broke it again in 1927. His record of 60 home runs in one season was the most famous record in baseball.

"The Babe," as he was called, could hit, run, field, throw, bat, and pitch. No other player has been so good at such a wide variety of skills. He could do anything in baseball.

1 **When did Babe Ruth hit exactly 54 home runs?**

    A   1920

    B   1921

    C   1922

    D   1927

Selection 2

The power of volcanoes has always fascinated and terrified people. Volcanoes are openings in the earth's surface from which lava, hot gases, and bits of rock erupt with great force. However, volcanoes begin deep within the earth. The heat is so great at certain depths inside the earth that the rock melts. This melted rock is called magma. As the rock melts, a gas also forms, and this gas-filled magma rises slowly upward. About two miles from the surface, it forms a chamber. From there it creates a passageway to the surface. When the magma nears the surface, the gas is released. The gas and magma blast out an opening, and a volcanic eruption occurs.

Once the magma has reached the surface, it is called lava. The lava is red-hot when it erupts from the opening, but it cools and hardens as it flows down the volcano and finally turns into rock. The volcano grows larger as more volcanic rock accumulates.

2 **What happens when the magma flows out of the opening of the volcano?**

A   It melts the rock.

B   It hardens on the side of the volcano.

C   It finds a weak spot in earth's surface.

D   It expands.

Selection 3

Some animals are predators. They hunt other animals, called prey, for their food. However, the prey have developed many different ways of protecting themselves from their predators.

Some are good at hiding and blend in with the background. When they sit still, their enemies can't find them. Stealth and camouflage may be the most common defense in the animal world. The antelope uses speed, another common defense, to stay away from the attacking lion. Good eyesight and a good sense of smell are vital to many other animals who don't want to serve as a predator's lunch.

There are many other techniques developed by prey animals. Porcupines have such sharp quills that most animals don't dare touch them. Skunks have the most unusual defense. They produce a bad smell that makes dangerous animals stay away.

Other animals, like the turtle, rely on their armor. When danger threatens, the turtle withdraws into its shell and is safe in its own portable castle.

3   **Which defense is LEAST commonly used?**

A   speed

B   camouflage

C   shells

D   bad smell

Selection 4

In this story, Ann is marrying Gilbert. While her marriage is a happy occasion, it also means she will be leaving her beloved home in Green Gables.

It was a happy and beautiful bride who came down the old homespun-carpeted stairs that September noon—the first bride of Green Gables, slender and shining-eyed, with her arms full of roses. Gilbert, waiting for her in the hall below, looked up at her with adoring eyes. She was his at last, this evasive, long-sought Anne, won after years of patient waiting. It was to him she was coming. Was he worthy of her? Could he make her as happy as he hoped? If he failed her—if he could not measure up to her standards...But then, their eyes met and all doubt was swept away in a glad certainty that everything would be wonderful. They belonged to each other; and, no matter what life might hold for them, it could never alter that. Their happiness was in each other's keeping and both were unafraid.

They were married in the sunshine of the old orchard, circled by the loving and kindly faces of long-familiar friends. Mr. Allan married them. Birds do not often sing in September, but one sang sweetly from some hidden tree while Gilbert and Anne repeated their vows. Anne heard it and thrilled to it. Gilbert heard it, and wondered only that all the birds in the world had not burst into jubilant song. The bird sang until the ceremony was ended. Then it wound up with one more little, glad trill. Never had the old gray green house among its enfolding orchards known a merrier afternoon. Laughter and joy had their way; and when Anne and Gilbert left to catch their train, Marilla stood at the gate and watched them drive out of sight down the long lane with its banks of goldenrod.

Anne turned at its end to wave her last goodbye. She was gone—Green Gables was her home no more.

—*From **Anne's House of Dreams** by L.M. Montgomery, Grosset and Dunlap, NY, 1917.*

4   **The bird began to sing—**

A   when Ann and Gilbert looked at each other

B   when Ann and Gilbert were married

C   when the ceremony ended

D   when Ann was given the roses

Selection 5

In 1635, Henry Morgan was born on a farm in Wales. When young, Henry decided to seek a life of adventure. Because life on a farm seemed dull to him, he left Wales for a life on the sea and became a professional pirate. He worked mainly on the Caribbean Sea, with the island of St. Catherine in the West Indies as his headquarters. His crew was made up of adventurers from all over the world.

Morgan made so much money as a pirate on the high seas that he decided he could afford to retire in splendor and luxury for the rest of his life. He settled on the island of Jamaica where, believe it or not, King Charles II of England appointed him lieutenant governor of Jamaica. The king knighted him, as well, making him Sir Henry Morgan. He remained a respected and important citizen of Jamaica until he died in 1688.

5   **Which detail belongs in the empty box?**

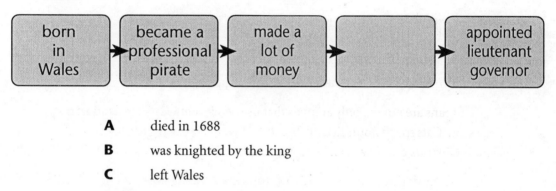

> born in Wales → became a professional pirate → made a lot of money → [ ] → appointed lieutenant governor

A   died in 1688

B   was knighted by the king

C   left Wales

D   retired

2. MAKING INFERENCES AND DRAWING CONCLUSIONS

We often make inferences or draw conclusions based on the information we have. If we see a policeman chasing someone, we might think that that person is a thief or has committed a crime. If we hear the sound of surf breaking, we might conclude that we are near the ocean. Our inferences may not always be correct, but they are the best guesses we can make from the information we have.

Read the example below and make the best inference you can.

Example 1

A deodorant destroys bad smells. A person who sweats a lot may use a deodorant. The deodorant makes the odor disappear.

Humans are not the only animals that use deodorants. Cats use deodorants every day. Cats spend hours licking their fur. Their saliva has a natural deodorant. That's why cats don't have an odor.

I love my dog but I wish she had a natural deodorant, too. Everyone can tell when she has ridden in the back of the car.

 1   **What can you infer from this selection?**

    A   Almost all animals have a natural deodorant.

    B   Cats often have an odor which some people dislike.

    C   Dogs often have an odor which some people dislike.

    D   When a cat rides in a car, the car gets a bad odor.

The correct answer is **Choice C**. You read that the author wishes her dog had a natural deodorant and that everyone can tell when she rode in the back of the car. You can guess that dogs often have an odor which some people dislike.

Sometimes you have to use everything you know to answer an inference-type question. Read Example 2. Try to figure out how Carlos changed.

Example 2

Carlos didn't really speak Spanish. His parents often spoke to him in that language, which he understood, but he always replied in English. As a result, his Spanish pronunciation was very bad, and he had trouble picking the right word. But then he fell in love with Alicia, who didn't understand English. Carlos changed very quickly.

2 **How did Carlos change?**

   A   He introduced Alicia to all his friends.

   B   He learned to speak Spanish better.

   C   He started to teach English to Alicia.

   D   He realized he couldn't get along with Alicia.

Your teacher will discuss your answer.

CAUSE AND EFFECT

We often make an inference when we try to understand why something happened. We try to understand the reason or cause for an event and also what effect it might have.

The word *because* often helps us understand why something happened.

Read the next selection and decide why Johnny's mother let him keep his pet snake.

Example 3

Johnny loved his pet snake, Pete, but his mother felt differently. She worried that the snake might get loose and that she would find it coiled up under her feet. The snake wasn't poisonous, but that didn't stop Johnny's mother from feeling anxious. However, because she loved her son, she let Johnny keep the snake anyway.

3 **Why did Johnny's mother let her son keep the snake?**

    A   She thought the snake was very valuable.

    B   She couldn't find another home for it.

    C   She wanted Johnny to be happy.

    D   She thought it would keep burglars away.

The correct choice is **C**. Johnny's mother loved her son. She wanted him to be happy. The selection uses the key word "because" and this helps you figure out the answer.

Some selections describe causes and effects without using key words like "because." Read Example 4 and decide why the starfish acts the way it does.

Example 4

The starfish hunts for clams in a strange way. When a starfish finds a clam, it wraps some of its arms around a rock and wraps the others around the clam. Then it pulls the clam open. After this, the starfish opens its mouth and pushes its stomach out of its mouth. The stomach goes into the clam shell and digests the clam. Then the starfish swallows its stomach again.

4 **Why do you think the starfish wraps its arms around a rock when it eats?**

    A   to help it digest its food

    B   to cool it down while it eats

    C   to anchor it firmly in place

    D   to obtain necessary minerals

The correct answer is **Choice C**. You must often make the best guess you can when you make an inference. In this selection, you can guess that the effect of the starfish wrapping some of its arms around a rock is that the starfish is anchored firmly so it can deal with the clam.

PREDICTING OUTCOMES

We can often make reasonable predictions based upon our understanding and knowledge of prior events.

Predict the most likely outcome in the next example.

Example 5

Every day after work, Harold went to visit his grandmother. He always arrived right at 5:25. His grandmother would have dinner waiting for him. Harold would leave her house exactly at 7:30 and go to his own home. He always went to sleep at 11 P.M. and got up at 7 in the morning. He always had the same breakfast—a bowl of cereal and a banana. He arrived at work by 8:30 and always had lunch at noon.

5 **Suppose Harold decided to take up jogging. When would you expect him to jog?**

   A   early in the morning

   B   whenever he felt like it

   C   at the same time every day

   D   in the afternoon

The best answer is **Choice C**. It is quite likely that Harold, who does everything at a set time, would also jog at the same time every day. Based on the information we know about him this is what we would predict. All the other choices are possible, but they are not the most probable.

STRATEGIES AND TIPS FOR MAKING INFERENCES AND PREDICTING OUTCOMES

1. When you are asked to make an inference, you must make a good guess. The correct answer is NOT written in the article.

2. Read the passage. Decide which answer makes the most sense. Then look at the choices. Make the best choice you can, even if you are not sure of the answer.

3. When you have to predict an outcome, ask yourself what is the main idea of the passage, or how do the people in a story behave for the most part. Then decide which answer choice is closest to your sense of the story and its characters.

SELECTIONS FOR PRACTICE

Selection 1

Plants need adequate amounts of water. Some of this water is used in photosynthesis, the process by which plants make food. However, most of it is used up in another way—by sweating. Plants sweat just as animals do.

Sweat is water that evaporates on the skin. Sweating is a process which cools the body. People sweat more in hot weather. Similarly, plants are cooled by evaporating water. Most of the water a plant takes in is used to keep it cool.

 1 **Which is probably true?**

A Plants need hot water.

B Plants need more water than animals.

C Plants use more water on hot days.

D Small plants need more water than large plants.

Selection 2

Grasshoppers deserve their name because their strong legs make them fine jumpers. Their back legs are very big; they use them to push off and leap into the air. Grasshoppers usually hop and fly only a little way at a time, but they can keep going for many miles. Grasshoppers also use their legs for singing! They rub their rear legs together making a scraping sound.

Grasshoppers like to eat almost anything that grows. Sometimes, many grasshoppers travel together and eat up entire fields at a time. They destroy crops and are difficult to control. Farmers don't like them, but children do because they are such fun to watch.

2   **Farmers don't like grasshoppers because**

    A   they make noise

    B   they eat crops

    C   they knock the crops down

    D   of their poisonous bite

Selection 3

Dr. Thomas walked up to Tyree in the waiting room. He spoke as gently as he could. "I'm sorry about Rover. We did everything we could to save him. But he was just too sick. I know how much you loved him. But I have something to show you."

Then Dr. Thomas showed Tyree a cute little puppy.

"No," the boy shouted. "I don't want to see your dog."

3   **The boy didn't want to see Dr. Thomas' puppy because**

    A   he was grieving over his dog Rover

    B   he didn't like puppies

    C   he thought the puppy was ugly

    D   he didn't want to take care of a dog

Selection 4

From about 1000 AD to the 1800's, Japan produced warriors who were among the bravest the world has ever known. These warriors were called samurai. The name samurai means "those who serve." The samurai served the nobles of Japan as soldiers in their armies and as personal bodyguards.

From earliest childhood, a samurai learned to ride horses and fight with swords. But more important was the mental training that the samurai received.

They were taught to give absolute loyalty to the lord they served. A samurai was expected to be more loyal to his lord than to his own family. If his lord asked it, the samurai would betray his family and even allow them to be killed.

A samurai was expected to fight to the death for his lord. Samurai believed it was an honor to die in battle. To these warriors, honor was more important than life itself. If a samurai shamed himself or his lord in some way, he was expected to ask permission to commit suicide. For example, if a samurai gave advice to his lord about how to fight a battle and the advice led to defeat, the samurai was shamed and he would ask his lord for permission to commit suicide.

Often the lord would refuse to let his loyal soldiers die. But the samurai had saved his honor by making the offer.

4   **What would a samurai probably do if a family member betrayed the samurai's lord?**

    A   allow the relative to be killed for his crime

    B   hide the relative from his lord's anger

    C   ask his lord to send him into battle to prove his loyalty

    D   leave Japan and never return

3. USING CONTEXT TO UNDERSTAND VOCABULARY

USING CONTEXT CLUES

I ransacked the bedroom.

What does the word *ransacked* mean? Unless you already know the word, you can't work out its meaning from the sentence. Now read this passage.

I took everything out of the drawers, looked under my bed, and searched the closet. I ransacked the entire bedroom, but I couldn't find my glasses.

If you read this passage carefully, you can figure out what *ransack* means. It means to search through something thoroughly. The words and sentences around it helped you to work out its meaning. You were able to figure out what ransack means from the context of the selection.

Read the next example and figure out the meaning of the word *sedentary*.

Example 1

I like my job typing medical records except for one thing. I find it very sedentary. I would rather have a job where I can move around more.

 1   **What does *sedentary* mean?**

    A   boring

    B   exhausting

    C   difficult to do

    D   not active

Choice D is correct. *Sedentary* means not active. When you read the selection you can figure out the meaning from the context clues. The selection tells you that the author would rather have a job that allowed him to move around more.

This clue helps you understand what *sedentary* means.

In the next example you will read about someone being *cordial*. The question doesn't ask you what the word means. Instead it will ask you to choose another example of cordial behavior.

Example 2

> The salesperson smiled when the couple came into the store. She told them to take their time in choosing a ring. She chatted with them about their future plans. She was the most cordial salesperson they had ever met.

 2   **Who else would be *cordial*?**

   A   someone who tells you to stop talking so loudly

   B   someone who enjoys romantic movies

   C   someone who feels no one should go to rock concerts

   D   someone who always says "Good Morning," and asks how you are doing

The correct choice is **D**. *Cordial* means being pleasant. The other choices are not examples of someone who is cordial.

There are many different ways to ask vocabulary questions. Sometimes you may be asked what a word means. But other times a selection may contain a difficult word. The question will not be directly about the word, but in order to answer it, you have to understand what the word means. Use context clues to figure out the meaning of the word.

Example 3

> Dorian developed a new scientific theory but none of his fellow scientists were impressed. Despite their rejection of his ideas, Dorian couldn't let it go. He kept insisting that his theory would work. He went everywhere to try to convince others that he should continue his project. Everyone else realized his work wouldn't succeed. But he wouldn't give it up. He didn't know when to stop.
>
> He was obsessed by the idea that he was right. Finally, he became so difficult to deal with that his friends didn't want to talk to him anymore. He lost his job.

3   **Which of the following people seem obsessed by something?**

   A   Latisha, who likes to work out for an hour three days a week

   B   Burt, who has a favorite Wednesday night TV show

   C   Carla, who spends 12 hours a day reading about chess

   D   Dave, who accidentally discovered an important antibiotic

To answer this question, you have to know the meaning of *obsessed*. Obsessed means being compulsive about something or someone to the point of not being reasonable. **Choice C** is correct.

PHRASES AND EXPRESSIONS

As you read, you sometimes come across single words you don't know. Or you may have trouble understanding phrases of two or more words.

For example, you might read the words "avalanche of sound." Read the next passage and work out the meaning of the phrase, "avalanche of sound."

Example 4

> The building was on fire. The heat and smoke were terrible. The sirens were going and people were screaming. Firemen were calling out to everyone. Horns were going off. Teri put her hands to her ears to keep out the noise. But she wouldn't leave the building. She didn't know if her cat was safe. It wasn't any use calling the cat's name because of the avalanche of sound all around her. All she could do was look for Cream in her favorite places.

4   **An "avalanche of sound" is**

   A   beautiful music

   B   a lot of loud noise

   C   easy to understand

   D   a very low level of sound

Your teacher will discuss your answer.

STATEGIES AND TIPS
FOR WORKING OUT
VOCABULARY MEANINGS

1.   Read the sentence with the new word.

2.   Read the sentences before and after this sentence.

3.   Take a guess at what the word probably means. Use a word that you think is a synonym to replace it in the sentence. See if it fits.

4.   Look at the answer choices. Pick the choice closest to what you guessed.

SELECTIONS FOR PRACTICE

Selection 1

All day long Diego kept thinking about Sue. For some unknown reason he was worried about her. He had a strong sense of foreboding that something was about to go wrong in Sue's city.

His fear was well-founded. Early the next morning, there was an earthquake. But fortunately, it was mild. Sue was shaken but unharmed.

1   A sense of *foreboding* is

    A   a feeling that something unfortunate may happen

    B   a feeling that you should be doing something else

    C   a feeling that you are popular

    D   a feeling that you have been misunderstood

Selection 2

Beverly is one of the most gregarious people I have ever known. She loves people, and spends a lot of her time talking to her friends and arranging get-togethers. She doesn't mind spending hours cooking as long as she knows that her house will be filled with people. She's just the opposite of her sister April, who never entertains.

2 *Gregarious* means

    A   easy to please

    B   difficult to get to know

    C   sociable

    D   unlikable

Selection 3

It was already May and Francesca still hadn't received her insurance money for the damage caused by the hurricane. She didn't know why it was taking so long. She had filled out all the paperwork and sent it back to the insurance company. She needed the money to pay the contractor to repair her house. When she called the insurance office, a woman said that the money would be disbursed by June 1. That made Francesca feel a lot better.

3   **What was going to happen by June 1?**

    A   Francesca was going to finish her paperwork.

    B   Francesca was going to call the insurance company.

    C   Francesca was going to receive her money.

    D   The contractor was going to pay Francesca.

Selection 4

The film company was making a movie and Tanya was the star. The movie was about how Tanya was captured by a dragon but managed to escape.

We watched them make the movie. Tanya had a large sword which she swung at an imaginary dragon and then jumped back. She acted like she was having a big fight, but there was nothing there.

Later Tanya described how they make the movie. She acts as if she is fighting a dragon; then later a computer synthesizes a picture of the creature. When the audience sees the film, they see Tanya fighting the dragon.

Tanya is the star of the movie, but the computer is just as important. The advertisements should say that the stars of the film are Tanya and the computer.

4 **How does the dragon get into the film?**

A It is filmed while he fights Tanya.

B It is created by the computer.

C It is painted on a white sheet.

D It is photographed in another film which is edited into this film.

Selection 5

Whenever Mia went to her grandparents' home, she liked to go to the basement to look around. There were all kinds of things stored there. Furniture, old papers, books, and things in little jars. Last week she opened a tin box and found a sparkling green gem. She thought it must be valuable and brought it upstairs to her grandfather. "When I was a young man those things were a dime a dozen," he told her. "They're still not worth anything." But Mia thought it was pretty and brought it home to put it on a shelf in her room.

5 **What else is a dime a dozen?**

A something that is rare

B something that is common

C something that won't break

D something that is colorful

4. DETERMINING THE MAIN IDEA AND THE DETAILS THAT SUPPORT IT

The **main idea** of a passage is what it is mostly about. It is what you would come up with if you had to summarize the selection in a single sentence.

Read the next passage. What is it mostly about?

Example 1

Elsie had always been fascinated by life in the early colonies. When she was 20, and studying history in college, she decided she wanted to see first hand what it was like to live in those days. She would try life without hot running water, electricity, telephones, and other modern conveniences.

During her summer vacation, Elsie discussed her decision with her family and they went along with it. Her father, a farmer, offered to help Elsie convert an old barn on the property. Together they made the barn into a simple, but livable, home. No TV, no electricity, but the colonists didn't have a bad life.

1 **What is the main idea of this passage?**

    A   finding out what it was like to live as a colonist

    B   finding out how to turn a chicken coop into a home

    C   why Elsie's father was a farmer

    D   how to live without running water

The correct choice is **A**. The author doesn't tell you this directly but you can figure it out from the details.

On the *New York State English Language Arts Test* you may be asked simply, "What is the main idea of this story?" Or the question might be asked in a different way. You might be asked, "What is the best title for the story?" or, "What is this story mostly about?" or, "What is the main topic of this story?"

Read Example 2 and answer the question.

Example 2

Looking for thrills and chills this winter? Hundreds of vacationers are heading for the wilderness in Yellowstone National Park, where they will take part in cross-country skiing tours sponsored by park officials and tour companies. The program began last winter, and it was so successful that it will be repeated this year. In the old days, only a few brave souls, most of them park rangers, were allowed to go into Yellowstone's back country in winter months. They traveled on skis or snowshoes, setting up camp at night. Those who survived the rugged journey told harrowing tales of being almost trapped in the snow or almost freezing to death. Some that ventured too far into the wilderness never returned. Today, people who go on the Yellowstone ski/camping tours can enjoy all the splendors of the back country with minimal risk. Trained guides, effective preparation, detailed maps, and modern equipment have greatly reduced the danger. Even people with no wilderness experience can sign up for a tour, provided they can ski and have the stamina for the long days spent gliding across the snowbound country.

2   **The best title for this selection is**

   A   "Getting Lost at Yellowstone National Park in the Winter"

   B   "Touring Yellowstone's Back Country in the Winter"

   C   "The Benefits of Cross-country Skiing"

   D   "Yellowstone's Trained Guides"

Choice B is correct, "Touring Yellowstone's Back Country in the Winter." This title describes what the selection is mostly about, its main idea. When a question asks for the best title of a selection, it is asking for the main idea.

THEME

In addition to a main idea, a story may have a **theme**. A theme is the message the author wants to deliver. It is a kind of lesson for life.

There are thousands of possible themes. A story theme might be something like:

> It is better to give than to receive.

Or it might be:

> Don't count on something until you get it.

Usually the author doesn't tell you what the theme is. You have to figure it out.

Example 3

My sister Emma and my brother Seymour both have perfect pitch. That means they can hear a note and sing it perfectly, even a week later. Many people sing well but Emma and Seymour do more than that—they never make a mistake.

My mother and father are both musicians and many of my cousins are just as gifted as Emma and Seymour. Musical ability seems to be commonplace in my family. Yet I can't sing on key. I even find it hard to tell if one note is higher than another. I just can't do it.

However, I can fix anything. My father and Seymour can't figure out how anything works. I just look at it and I understand it right away. I took apart a big clock and cleaned it when I was six. Seymour couldn't even figure out how to take off the case.

3 **What lesson can the reader learn from this story?**

A People have different abilities.

B Musical ability makes life enjoyable.

C Some people can never learn to sing.

D Friends may disagree.

The correct choice is **A**, People have different abilities. That is the main point of the story. The other choices are incorrect.

SUPPORTING DETAILS

Supporting details help to describe the main idea of a passage. Some supporting details are examples of the main idea.

Passages and paragraphs often start with a main idea. Then the rest of the passage has details about that idea or examples of it.

The next selection is filled with information about refinishing a piece of furniture.

Example 4

Even though it is a lot of work, you can save yourself and your family a lot of money if you learn how to refinish furniture. When you refinish a piece of furniture, you get rid of all the marks and scratches that have accumulated over the years. Your furniture looks like new. You can also give it a different look by changing the color of the stain, paint, or varnish. Once you know the basic steps, the possibilities are endless, and the chances are you will never throw out your old furniture again. When refinishing, remember to have proper ventilation whenever you use stripper, paint, or varnish. It's probably best to do the refinishing out-of-doors or in a shed whenever possible.

4 **Which detail explains why refinishing is a satisfying way to improve old furniture?**

 A Your furniture will look like new.

 B Refinishing is a lot of work.

 C Make sure to have proper ventilation when using stripper, paint, or varnish.

 D It's best to do the refinishing out-of-doors or in a shed.

The correct answer is **A**. This detail supports the main idea. The other choices do not.

USING GRAPHIC ORGANIZERS TO DETERMINE MAIN IDEAS AND SUPPORTING DETAILS

A type of graphic organizer called **webbing** uses a circle surrounded by boxes.

• The circle in the middle usually contains a main idea.

• The other boxes have details about this idea.

This kind of graphic is used in the next example. Read the passage. Then look at the organizer.

Example 5

I grew up in a big city. Kids back then played a lot of street games. But most of these games have died out now.

When I was 12, every guy played stickball. You just needed a broomstick and a rubber ball. We played for a couple of hours every day. When we weren't playing stickball, we played box ball and stoop ball. Kids today have never heard of these old games.

We were on bikes a lot and we played handball and basketball; they are about the only games still left. We did have roller skates, but they weren't fancy like today's skates. In-line skates and skateboards didn't exist. And our sneakers weren't very fancy and didn't cost much. Even the richest kids in the neighborhood didn't have the kind of sneakers that kids wear today.

Girls don't play hopscotch much anymore, but they still jump rope. I see my daughter's friends jumping double dutch out on the street after school. But my two younger daughters are always playing softball. Few women played softball 20 years ago. And my oldest daughter is skilled at karate. She now has a black belt, second degree. Women didn't practice the martial arts either when I was growing up.

5   **What detail belongs in Box 4?**

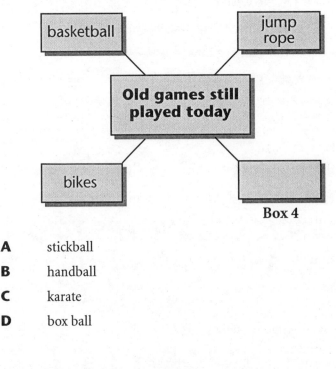

A   stickball

B   handball

C   karate

D   box ball

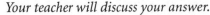 *Your teacher will discuss your answer.*

STRATEGIES AND TIPS FOR FINDING THEMES AND MAIN IDEAS, AND THE DETAILS THAT SUPPORT THEM

1. After you read a selection, ask yourself, "What was the story about?" Try to sum up your answer in a single sentence.

2. Don't confuse a story detail with the main idea. Details tell you more about the main idea.

3. Look out for a "lesson for life" that the story teaches. A "lesson for life" is the theme or message of the story.

4. Make sure that the theme is one that the story teaches. Don't choose a theme that sounds good but has nothing to do with the actual story.

5. To complete a main idea/supporting detail graphic:
   - If the center box is empty, you must find the main idea.
     + Check the details in the outside boxes.
     + Decide what main idea they support.
   - If an outside box is empty, you must find a supporting detail.
     + Read the main idea in the center box.
     + Decide which details in the story support that idea.
     + Find a detail that does not appear in another box.

SELECTIONS FOR PRACTICE

Selection 1

Most of the native civilizations of South America disappeared after the arrival of Europeans in the 16th century. However, a few tribes have survived and prospered to the present day. One of these is the Guajiro tribe of Venezuela, which occupies the Guajiro Peninsula, the northern tip of South America.

The Guajiro Indians number about 100,000. The social system of the Guajiro tribe is based on a matrilineal pattern—descent is traced from the mother's side of the family, not the father's. For example, a father leaves his property to his sister's children, although he is expected to provide for his own children during his lifetime. Also, a man must buy a wife and live near his wife's relatives. The Guajiro way of life is very different from that of most people in Venezuela, but they show no signs of wishing to abandon it.

1A **What is the most important thing you learn from this passage?**

    A   Why most of the Indian civilizations in South America disappeared

    B   Why a Guajiro man must buy a wife

    C   The fact that the Guajiro Indians still practice their traditional way of life

    D   That a large number of Guajiro Indians still exist

1B **What detail supports the main idea?**

    A   The Guajiro Indians number about 100,000.

    B   Most Indian civilizations of South America disappeared after the arrival of Europeans in the 16th century.

    C   A Guajiro father leaves his property to his sister's children.

    D   The Guajiro tribe is located in Venezuela.

Selection 2

Ataya was happy. She had just been to an audition for the starring role in the school play and she felt sure she'd got the part. It was a part she loved and she knew she would be perfect in the role. After the audition, she told her friends she would be starring in the play. She told them to make sure they bought tickets when the show opened. She called her mother and told her the good news. And she talked to the high school newspaper editor about the meaning of the play.

Then on Tuesday the director called and told her they had decided to offer the part to Monica Quarles. He offered Ataya a tiny role. She put down the phone in tears.

2 **What lesson does this story teach?**

    A   Acting is a difficult job.

    B   Never try out for a role that you like.

    C   Never count on something until it happens.

    D   Don't tell your mother all your secrets.

Selection 3

Almost all American homes are heated by oil or gas. Both methods are expensive and add to environmental pollution. Because of this, engineers and architects are constantly looking for new ways to provide more energy-efficient housing. One experimental house, built in New Canaan, Connecticut, requires little energy for heating. The house was half buried in the ground and relies on the heat that is stored beneath the earth's surface. The underground temperature in New Canaan remains at 52° throughout the year even when the temperature above ground is below freezing. This natural source of heat is apparent in other underground structures, such as subway stations or basements. Even in the coldest winter months, those areas are warmer than rooms built above the ground. However, before this house was built, no one had thought to use the earth's heat to the extent that it was used in this experimental home.

3   **The best title for this selection is**

A   "Underground Structures"

B   "A Natural Source of Heat"

C   "Housing in Connecticut"

D   "Using Oil or Gas for Heating"

Selection 4

A football quarterback must have an amazing collection of skills. First of all, under pressure, he must be able to make split-second decisions. He must be able to judge what is happening downfield, decide where to pass or run, and do this when strong, determined opponents are hurtling at him. He must have the ability to throw accurately, to run with speed and agility, and to change plays at the last moment.

And he must be able to play day after day, despite a collection of injuries that would leave the average person in pain and agony. Football is a tough game with a lot of fierce contact, and much of the defensive effort of the much bigger tacklers is aimed at bringing down the quarterback. Few quarterbacks have escaped knee and shoulder injuries, twisted ankles, broken ribs, and so on—and yet they are often able to keep playing despite their injuries.

No championship team in the National Football League has ever succeeded without a great quarterback.

4   **Look at the graphic. Select the information that belongs inside Box 3.**

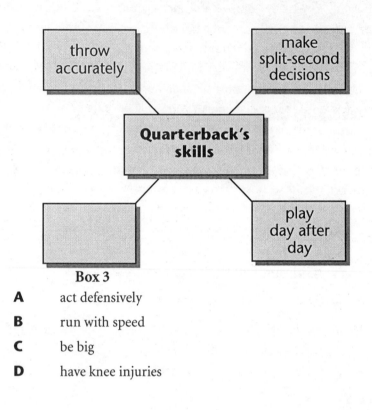

Box 3

A   act defensively

B   run with speed

C   be big

D   have knee injuries

5. ANALYZING STORY PLOTS

PROBLEMS AND RESOLUTIONS

Most fictional narratives contain **plots**. In a typical plot, there is a central problem; something goes wrong. The story may also provide a resolution—how the problem is dealt with or solved.

Suppose you read a story about a young boy who couldn't find his mother in a big department store. You might learn how he got lost and how afraid he felt. Then you might read that another customer helped the boy to find his mother. This story has a very simple plot. But it still has a central problem—a child is lost. And it has a resolution—the child finds his mother again.

Read the next example. Notice how each event helps to develop the plot. Decide on the problem in this passage and how it is resolved.

Example 1

Rosa loved to play baseball until one day when she was hit by a ball. The ball struck her on the shoulder and she was in pain for many hours. After that, she refused to play again—she was too scared to enjoy the game. Rosa decided her baseball-playing days were over.

About a year later, Rosa was watching her friends play baseball. The sun was shining and everyone was having a good time. She felt depressed. She wished she could join in. Suddenly Rosa realized that there was really no reason she shouldn't play, too, even if she was afraid. A little tentatively, she joined in the game and soon she was enjoying herself immensely.

1A **What caused the central problem in this story?**

A Rosa was depressed when she sees others playing ball.

B Rosa was frightened to play baseball.

C Rosa loved to play baseball.

D The sun was shining.

The correct choice is **B**. The central problem of this story begins when Rosa is hit by a ball and becomes too frightened to play baseball. The other three choices contain something you read in the story. But none of them describes the central problem.

You might also be asked about the resolution of the story.

1B   **How was this problem resolved?**

    A   Rosa didn't play after she was hit.

    B   Rosa learned to enjoy watching her friends play ball.

    C   Rosa played ball again, even though she was scared.

    D   Rosa stopped watching baseball games.

The correct choice is **C**. Despite her fear, Rosa played baseball again and loved it. Choice D is not correct. We aren't told this—it isn't even implied or suggested. Choice B is incorrect, too. Rosa didn't enjoy seeing her friends play ball. This made her unhappy. Choice A is wrong. Rosa stopped playing ball after she was hit. But that was the central problem, not how the problem was resolved.

A fictional narrative that contained only one problem and its resolution would be dull indeed. Authors include details to provide interest and color. They paint verbal pictures of the actors in their stories. In the story of Rosa, the baseball player, you learned details of her personal history and how she responded to an accident.

Questions about the plot of a story are expressed in different ways. Read the next example and answer the questions.

Example 2

Ricci and Frances worked in New York City. They were offered better jobs upstate in Woodstock. Their mechanic, Mark, said he would have the van fixed and ready to move them in three weeks. So they decided to quit their old jobs and take a vacation before starting the new ones.

But when they came back from vacation, the van wasn't ready. Mark said he was waiting for a special part. And he said that if the part wasn't there in three days, he wouldn't be able to finish the job before he went away on vacation.

Ricci called the dealer. He told him to air express the part. Two days later the special package arrived and the van was finally fixed.

2A   Ricci's and Frances' van wasn't fixed when they came back from vacation because

    A   they had quit their jobs

    B   they were moving upstate

    C   the mechanic was on vacation

    D   the mechanic needed a special part

    Your teacher will discuss your answer.

Read the next question.

2B   **How is this problem resolved?**

    A   Ricci and Frances took new jobs in Woodstock.

    B   Ricci and Frances came back from vacation.

    C   Mark went on vacation.

    D   Mark received the part.

The correct choice is **D**. Mark received the part and fixed the van. That is the resolution to the central problem.

STRATEGIES AND TIPS FOR WORKING OUT A STORY'S PLOT

1.   Try to figure out the *central problem* or *conflict* in a passage. See if you can find the event that caused this problem.

2.   Notice how a story ends. Many stories end by resolving their central problems.

SELECTIONS FOR PRACTICE

Selection 1

On Tuesday, Emily walked into her biology class and saw her teacher passing out the exam sheet. "Uh, oh," she said to herself, as she sat down. She quickly looked at her notes before Mrs. Lambert told the students to put them away and open the test. After school that day, Emily went to see her teacher. "I'm afraid I wasn't ready for the exam," she told Mrs. Lambert. Mrs. Lambert had just finished grading the tests. "You didn't do very well. Didn't you study?" Emily looked crestfallen. She began to say something, but her voice trailed off. "I just had so much to do…."

"I understand your mother has been sick," Mrs. Lambert said. "I ran into your father and he said she had been in the hospital for a week. And he said that you've been taking care of the family. He was very proud of you," said Mrs. Lambert. "I can't ignore the grade, but if you come to see me ninth period, perhaps you could make up some extra credit by doing another lab. How's that sound?" she asked.

"Oh, Mrs. Lambert. Thank you so much. I'll be there," Emily answered, a smile on her face.

1A **What problem did Emily have?**

A   Mrs. Lambert gave a biology test.

B   Emily didn't do well on the biology test.

C   Mrs. Lambert ran into Emily's father.

D   Mrs. Lambert finished grading the tests.

1B **What did Mrs. Lambert do to make Emily smile?**

A   She told Emily her test grade wasn't very good.

B   She told Emily that she could make up extra credit.

C   She asked Emily whether she studied for the test.

D   She told Emily her father was proud of her.

Selection 2

Daphne and Marika had been friends for a long time, ever since they were in elementary school. They both liked to ice skate and they usually went to the gym together. Often they would run together in the morning before school. For the past week, whenever Daphne came by her house, Marika would say she didn't feel like going to the gym. She told Daphne that she just couldn't get out of bed early enough to go for a run.

Daphne wondered why her friend was so different. On Saturday, while she was out for a run, she was sure she spotted Marika walking in the other direction across the street with Pamela. What made it worse was that it was Daphne's birthday. Daphne felt confused. Later that day, she went to the movies with her sister Tanya. They were supposed to meet their family at 6 o'clock for a special family celebration at the lake. It was a nice treat, but it wasn't enough to make Daphne forget that Marika hadn't called her first thing in the morning to wish her a happy birthday like she always had done in the past. And, she thought, this will be the first time that Marika hadn't given her a present.

When they got to the lake, her parents already had the fire going in the barbecue. Her brother Ted was there and so were her cousins Bob and Anna. She sat down and looked into the water. There reflected in the water was Marika. She turned around. "Surprise," Marika cried out. Behind her were a bunch of her friends and they were smiling and laughing. They all had presents and balloons.

"I wanted to really surprise you," Marika told her. "I knew if I saw you I would give it away."

2A	**Why does Daphne feel confused?**
A	She went out for a run.
B	Saturday is her birthday.
C	Marika doesn't run with her.
D	Marika liked to ice skate.

2B	**How is Daphne's problem resolved?**
A	She goes to the movies.
B	Her family is having a barbecue for her.
C	Marika doesn't like to run anymore.
D	Marika surprises Daphne with a party.

6. ANALYZING CHARACTERS

In order to understand a story, you must understand the people in it. The **characters** in a story give it meaning.

Read Example 1 and decide who is the most important character in the story.

Example 1

Alma Way stared straight ahead. Her long, delicate face was pale. Her gloved hands, clutching the hymn book, trembled as she sang. The time for her solo was near. She felt panic rising within her but she took a deep breath. Then her voice rang out, clear as a bell. The congregation nodded admiringly. Suddenly there was another sound. All the faces turned towards the windows on the south side of the church. Above the rasp of the wind and the birds, high above Alma Way's sweetly straining tones, rose another female voice, singing another hymn to another tune. It was Candace Whitcomb, who had recently been dismissed as the solo singer at the church. After the service, the minister spoke to Alma, and told her how much he regretted the incident.

1A	Who is the most important character in the story?

    A   Alma Way

    B   Candace Whitcomb

    C   churchgoers

    D   the minister

A is the correct choice. All of the choices are in the story, but Alma Way is the most important character because the author tells us most about her.

1B Alma Way was

A extremely confident

B difficult to deal with

C nervous but determined

D upset with the minister

The correct choice is **C**. The selection says that Alma Way was pale, that her hands trembled, but that she sang out clear as a bell. The other choices are incorrect.

You usually learn a lot about the important characters in a story. Authors describe them carefully.

One way to describe someone is to use adjectives, like "lively" or "cheerful" or "independent" or "fearful." Another way is to describe how the person acts. You can usually figure out what people are like from the way they act.

Example 2

When the meeting was over, Satoshi returned to his desk in a daze. He didn't know if he was going to break down and cry. The news had come as such a surprise. He never dreamed that he could lose his job. He couldn't decide whether to tell anyone or just keep it to himself for a while. He didn't know whether to go directly home or take a long walk to calm himself.

2 **How would you describe Satoshi?**

A pleased with himself

B shocked and confused

C angry with his boss

D tired

Your teacher will discuss your answer.

HOW CHARACTERS CHANGE

Sometimes you are asked how a character changes during the course of a story.

Read Example 3 and decide how Ben changes.

Example 3

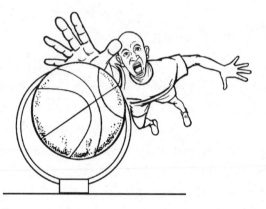

Ben didn't spend much time studying—he found other things more interesting than school work. He loved playing basketball. He loved the movies, especially martial arts films. He was just beginning to study Aikido and got a big kick out of it. And he got the highest score on the Midnight Jazz video game, better than guys who were a lot older.

Ben's parents had a serious talk with him after he flunked a science test. He promised he'd study more, but he just didn't get around to it. Last month, Ben went to see his guidance counselor, Mr. Aidala, to see which school Ben should go to after graduation. Mr. Aidala liked Ben, and they often joked around with each other. But when Mr. Aidala looked at Ben's record, he became very serious. He told Ben that if he wanted to do well in high school and get into a good college he would have to do a lot better. Ben didn't say anything, but that evening he spent three hours doing his homework. He started studying every night. Last week he got a 91 on his science test and an A on his English composition.

3   **How did Ben change?**

    A   He began to spend more time on basketball.

    B   He decided to enjoy life more.

    C   He started studying more.

    D   He worked harder at video games.

The correct answer is **Choice C**. Ben started to study more and got better grades. The selection doesn't mention that he worked harder at video games or that he began to spend more time on basketball or that he decided to enjoy life more.

USING GRAPHIC ORGANIZERS TO ANALYZE CHARACTERS

Graphic organizers can be used to help us analyze characters. Read the next selection and look at the graphic organizer.

Example 4

Gregory was a computer programmer. He worked hard all week long. But on weekends he liked to relax. Every Saturday during the summer when it was nice out, Gregory went to the park. He liked to go to the zoo and see the elephants and llamas too. He would often invite a friend from the place where he worked and bring a picnic lunch with him. He would sit on the hill overlooking the ballfield and watch the kids play. On Saturdays when it was raining he would go to the movies. Gregory liked to do the same things at the same time. He thought it was fun.

Character Trait	Supporting Details
liked to do the same things at the same time	went to park every Saturday sat on hill overlooking ballfield _____

4   **What other supporting detail belongs on the empty line?**

    A   was computer programmer

    B   had friends

    C   went to movies when it rained

    D   worked hard

The correct choice is **C**. This detail supports Gregory's character trait of liking to do the same things at the same time. The others are all things about Gregory, but they do not support the character trait.

The following selections are filled with people. As you read, notice what these people look like and what kinds of people they are. Pay attention to how they behave. Try to understand why they behave the way they do.

STRATEGIES AND TIPS FOR UNDERSTANDING A CHARACTER IN A STORY

1. A character is a person in a story. Look for parts of the story that tell you how the character acts.

2. Decide which word or words describe the character.

3. Sometimes there are two characters in the story. Decide how they are alike and how they are different.

SELECTIONS FOR PRACTICE

Selection 1

This selection comes from a play written by Eugene O'Neill, one of America's best-known playwrights. It was written in 1921. In it, Anna tells her friend Marthy about her life as a child. After her mother died, her father sent her to work on a farm.

Anna: (Angrily)His bringing me up! Is that what he tells people! I like his nerve. He let those cousins of my Old Woman keep me on their farm and work me to death like a dog.

Marthy: Well, he's got queer notions. I've heard him say a farm is the best place for a kid.

Anna: Sure. That's what he'd always answer back. He was a monster!

Marthy: (Casually) So you didn't fall for life on the farm, Huh?

Anna: I should say not! The old man of the family, his wife, and four sons—I had to slave for all of them. I was only a poor relation, and they treated me worse than they'd treat a hired girl.

1   **Anna's attitude towards her early life is**

A   grateful for what she had

B   angry and resentful

C   amused

D   sympathetic to the people she knew well

Selection 2

The professor looked up at Dr. Farrar, fumbling with a pile of papers. "Farrar, what's the matter with you?" he said sharply.

The younger man started. "Why...why...." The brusqueness of the other's manners shocked him suddenly into confession. "I've lost my nerve, Professor Mallory; that what's the matter with me. I'm frightened to death," he said melodramatically.

"What of?" asked Mallory, with a little challenge in his tone.

The floodgates were open. The younger man burst out in exclamations, waving his thin, nervous, knotted fingers, his face twitching as he spoke.

"This virus, Professor. We've had four deaths in the hospital this week. It's deadly. And we don't have any medication to control it. I don't know what to do for my patients. I'm terrified I might get it myself."

"Yes, it's frightening and unbearable to watch people grow sicker and not be able to help. But we must keep working. We must take precautions and continue our work. We have learned to cure many illnesses. I have faith we will overcome this virus, too. You have to get hold of yourself and continue on."

2	**How does Professor Mallory compare to Farrar?**

    A   Professor Mallory is calmer.

    B   Professor Mallory is less mature.

    C   Professor Mallory is sicker.

    D   Professor Mallory is more melodramatic.

Selection 3

In this story a woman prepares to go to a ball and is upset because she has no jewels to wear. It is written by a famous French writer, Guy DeMaupassant.

The day of the ball drew near, and Madame Loisel seemed sad, uneasy, anxious. Her dress was ready, however. Her husband said to her one evening:

"What is the matter? Come, you've been so strange these last three days."

And she answered:

"It annoys me not to have a single jewel, not a single stone, nothing to put on. I shall look so wretched. I should almost rather not go at all."

He resumed:

"You might wear natural flowers. It's very stylish at this time of the year. For ten francs you can get two or three magnificent roses."

She was not convinced.

"No; there's nothing more humiliating than to look poor among other women who are rich."

But her husband cried:

"How silly you are! Go look up your friend Madame Forestier, and ask her to lend you some jewels. You're quite thick enough with her to do that."

She uttered a cry of joy:

"That's true. I never thought of it."

3A   **What is Madame Loisel's problem?**

   A   She doesn't have a dress to wear to the ball.

   B   She hates flowers.

   C   She doesn't have jewels to wear to the ball.

   D   She feels uneasy.

3B   **What word best describes Madame Loisel's personality?**

   A   self-confident

   B   dissatisfied

   C   cheerful

   D   timid

Selection 4

Genia was very proud of her hair. It was a rich chestnut color with flecks of red and it curled naturally around her face and neck. She liked to brush her hair at night until it shined. She usually wore it back with the two gold combs her mother had given her for Christmas.

Genia had wanted to join the army ever since she was a little girl. In her senior year at high school she decided to sign up. She was very excited to learn that she would be going to California for training. When she arrived, she stood in line with all the new recruits. They were given uniforms and then they had to have their hair cut. Usually Genia had no difficulty in following orders. As she stepped up to the barber's chair, she hesitated. Finally she sat down. As she saw her long tresses dropping to the floor, she had to stifle a sob.

Character Trait	Supporting Details
proud of hair	liked to brush hair wore golden combs _____

4 **What other supporting detail belongs on the empty line?**

    A   followed orders

    B   sobbed when hair was cut

    C   stood in line with new recruits

    D   signed up for army senior year

7. COMPARING AND CONTRASTING

USING GRAPHIC ORGANIZERS TO COMPARE AND CONTRAST

Graphic organizers can help you compare people, things, or ideas.

Suppose, for example, that you were asked to describe the differences between pizza and hot dogs. To make a graphic organizer, you would draw two columns like the ones below, one headed Pizza and the other headed Hot Dog. In the Pizza column, you would write down what is true about pizza but not about hot dogs. Then you would do the same thing about hot dogs in the Hot Dog column. When your graphic organizer was finished, you would be able to see at a glance how you might answer the original question.

Pizza	Hot Dog
has crust	usually served in roll
usually round shape	usually long and thin in shape
topped with sauce and cheese	topped with mustard or sauerkraut

In the next example, you will read about Aileen and Yolanda. Read the passage. Then decide how the girls are different. Don't try to use complete sentences. Use short phrases to describe their differences.

Example 1

Aileen was tall and lanky, studied hard, got all A's and hardly ever talked in class. Yolanda was short and thin, cracked jokes all the time and barely passed exams. Yet the two girls were best friends. They went to the school cafeteria together, went to the basketball games together, and were rarely apart. They even used the same expressions when they talked. Most of their friends joked about how much time they spent together and even called them "the Siamese Twins." So it was difficult for Aileen when Yolanda's family suddenly moved away. She didn't have anyone to go to the movies with. She didn't have anyone to hang out with. And for the first time in her life, she failed a math quiz.

1   How do Aileen and Yolanda differ from each other? Fill in the chart to show their differences. Use your own words.

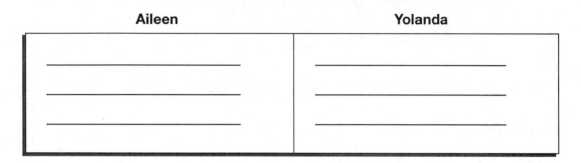

Aileen	Yolanda
_____	_____
_____	_____
_____	_____

Now look at how one student answered this question:

Aileen	Yolanda
tall and lanky	short and thin
got all A's	cracked jokes
rarely talked in class	barely passed exams

This student has listed the details that make Aileen different from Yolanda.

Sometimes you will be asked how people or things are the same as well as how they are different. You can use another kind of graphic organizer to show this. It is called a Venn diagram.

The Venn diagram below shows how the Aileen and Yolanda are similar as well as how they are different.

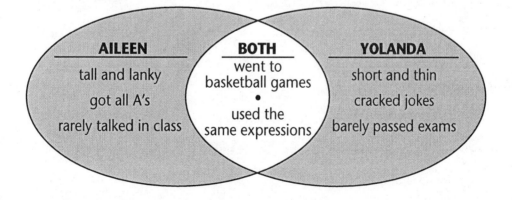

Notice that the diagram has two circles with a place in the middle where they overlap.

- In the parts of the circles that don't overlap, you list the differences between the twins.

- In the overlapping part, you list the things they have in common.

Read this passage about Barry and Boris. Then study the diagram that shows how the two men differed and how they were similar. Complete the diagram by finding something else the two men had in common.

Example 2

Barry and Boris were friends. Barry was born in New York City, and Boris was born in Russia. Boris came to the United States when he was 21 and the two men became friends. They enjoyed the same sports, and they and their wives liked the same movies. Barry loved to take long walks, and so did Boris. They would spend several hours a week walking along the avenues and window shopping, looking at all the people and talking about their lives and their futures. Barry sometimes felt worried when they had to cross a street. Boris ignored traffic rules. He was as likely to cross in the middle of the block as at the corners, and he was indifferent to whether the light was green or red. He walked across the street between cars as if he were a football star escaping from would-be tacklers. Twice he was almost hit by cabs.

Barry asked Boris why he didn't cross with the light. Boris said, "I know how Americans cross and it's ridiculous. In my old country, no man is afraid of cars."

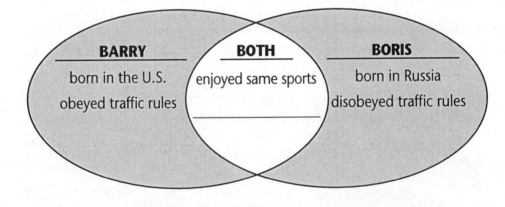

2 There are other details you could put in the overlapping part. Can you figure out what one of them is?

 Your teacher will discuss your answer

COMPARING CHARACTERS

When the **New York State English Language Arts Test** asks you about a character, it will usually ask you to compare one person with another. Try to see in what ways characters are alike and in what ways they are different. How the characters differ from each other may be an important part of the story.

Read the next example and compare Fernando and Philippe.

Example 3

Fernando was very hard to get to know. He didn't like to talk on the telephone. He hardly went out to parties. He liked to stay home and practice the piano. Philippe, his brother, loved to be outdoors. He played baseball and ice hockey, and had a lot of friends. He was always concerned about Fernando and told him that he should get out more. He invited him to go to football games with his friends. He asked him to come hiking with him on weekends.

Sometimes Fernando would accept, but he hardly ever enjoyed himself. He said he'd rather be at home, learning a new musical piece. This made Philippe sad. He worried that his brother was all work and no play.

Many years later, Fernando became a successful musician. When the two men got together, they would laugh about how worried Philippe had been about his "lonely" brother.

3 **How did Fernando differ from Philippe?**

   A   He liked to hike.

   B   He enjoyed playing the piano.

   C   He was good at ice hockey.

   D   He was older.

The correct answer is **Choice B**. Fernando enjoyed playing the piano. Choices A and C describe Philippe not Fernando. The selection does not say which brother was older.

COMPARING SETTINGS

A setting is the time and place in which a story takes place. A story may take place in more than one place.

Sometimes you are asked to compare two settings.

Read Example 4.

Example 4

Inside the fire burned brightly. The aroma of a roast cooking in the oven filled the air. He could hear his wife and children in the next room. They were playing a board game. He sat on the couch and looked around at the colorful paintings that decorated the walls. This was his favorite room in the whole house.

He saw that the fire was burning down and put on his jacket. As he opened the door, the cold hit him like a train. His breath looked like puffs of clouds. Everything was very white. He stomped along the snowy path to the wood pile, took the cover off, and pulled out several logs. It was going to be a long winter.

4   **How did the outdoors differ from inside the house?**

    A   It was more comfortable.

    B   It was warmer.

    C   It was colder.

    D   It was more colorful.

 Your teacher will discuss your answer.

INTERPRETING AND COMPARING MAPS

The **New York State English Language Arts Test** may ask you information about a map or to compare two maps and answer a question based on the information found in the maps and in the text that is given to you.

Example 5

The modern steam engine was invented in 1769 by the Scottish engineer and inventor James Watt. In 1804, an American inventor named Oliver Evans said that he believed he could create a steam carriage that would run 15 miles an hour on level railways. Then in 1812 Colonel John Stevens, of Hoboken, N.J., began to envision a railway that would furnish long-range transportation, linking distant sections of the nation. Ultimately the railroad had far reaching impact on the way people and goods were transported.

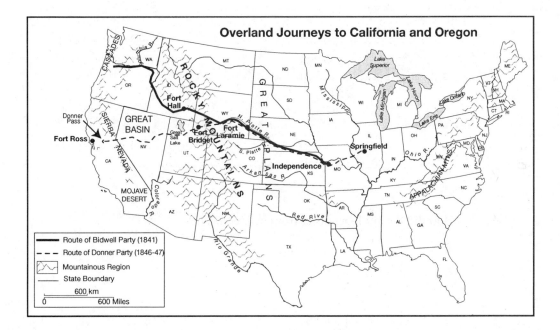

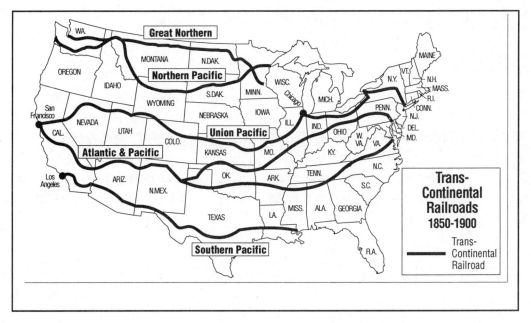

5 **Study the text and the maps. What kind of impact did the invention of the steam engine have on transportation in the 1800's?**

    A   People could bring more belongings with them on the railroad

    B   Railroads made it easier and faster to travel to California.

    C   Railroads made traveling very expensive.

    D   Rivers were used more often than before for travel.

If you study the maps closely, you can figure out that Choice **B** is correct.

STRATEGIES AND TIPS FOR MAKING COMPARISONS AND CONTRASTS

1.   See if a chart or a Venn diagram would help you to decide how things are alike and how they differ.

2.   Read the captions and keys on maps carefully. Make sure you understand what all the symbols mean and what geographic area and time period each map covers.

SELECTIONS FOR PRACTICE

Selection 1

Bernard loved to paint. He regularly put in eight hours a day at his craft. He worked six days a week. His sister Keisha was an actress. On days that she performed or rehearsed, she put in very long hours. Sometimes she worked 14 or 16 hours a day. But then she would not work for months in between jobs. Keisha was always surrounded by dozens of friends. Bernard was also popular, but he preferred to spend his time quietly. They both had successful careers.

1 Some of the information about Bernard and Keisha is filled in for you. Find two things they had in common. Fill in the empty boxes.

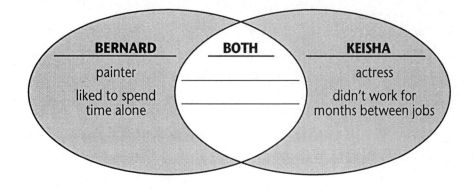

BERNARD	BOTH	KEISHA
painter		actress
liked to spend time alone		didn't work for months between jobs

Selection 2

"Is it a robber?" whispered Sasha.

"It is not a man. I see his head; it is a bear. Keep quiet, boy! Make no noise. Take this tough stick but hold it at your side, as I do with mine. Look him in the face, if he comes close; and if I tell you to strike, hit him on the end of the nose."

It was, indeed, a full-grown bear, marching slowly on his great flat feet. He was not more than thirty yards distant, when he saw them, and stopped. Both kept their eyes fixed upon his head, but did not move. The bear gazed steadily at them for what seemed a long time. Finally he gave a sniff and a grunt, tossed up his nose, and slowly walked on, stopping once or twice to turn and look back, before he disappeared from view. Sasha lifted his stick and shook it towards him; he felt that he would never again be much afraid of bears.

"Now boy," said Gregor, "you have learned how to face danger."

—*From "Boys of Other Countries," by Bayard Taylor, American Book Company, 1911.*

2 **How does Sasha differ from Gregor?**

A Sasha is older and wiser than Gregor.

B Sasha likes bears more than Gregor.

C Gregor is less fearful than Sasha.

D Gregor doesn't like animals of any kind.

Selection 3

On the exterior it looked tidy and pleasant—a little log cabin with a fence around it. The lawn was cut close and the bushes were all tended to. No weeds in this yard. Inside was another story. The furniture was covered with dust. Huge spider webs dangled from the ceiling, and the floor was covered with dirt. It would take quite a bit of effort to make this into their dream vacation home, but they decided to try.

3   **How did the exterior of the cabin compare to the interior?**

    A   The exterior was messier.

    B   The exterior was neater.

    C   The interior was cleaner.

    D   The interior was less in need of work.

Selection 4

New York State was originally settled by the Dutch in the early 1600's after Henry Hudson's historic trip in his ship, *The Half Moon*, in 1609 up the river which bears his name today. Even though his explorations ended tragically when his men mutinied, the rich Hudson Valley attracted many Dutch farmers earning them the reputation of being the breadbasket of the entire region. The Dutch were by no means the only settlers in New York. By the 1700's, the Middle Colonies were a melting pot of various nationalities.

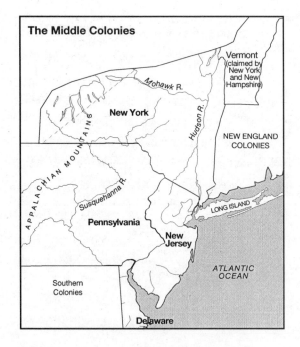

4   **Study the text and the maps. Where did the majority of Dutch settlers live?**

    A   in Northern New York State

    B   on Long Island

    C   in western Pennsylvania

    D   along the Hudson River corridor

8. IDENTIFYING THE AUTHOR'S VIEWPOINT AND PURPOSE

AUTHOR'S VIEWPOINT

An author's **viewpoint** about a subject influences what he or she writes.

In the following example, decide what the author feels about television.

Example 1

Fifty years ago, there was no TV. After dinner, families would often play games together, or possibly take a walk. Sometimes they had long discussions about what was important to them. And sometimes they would sit around the radio and listen to mystery shows and comedy shows.

Usually families had only one radio, so everyone listened to the same show. When television was invented, all that began to change. Today, instead of sitting together, most family members now go to their separate rooms to watch the TV shows they want to see. There is very little interaction between family members, and more and more families never do anything together in the evening.

All this has a bad impact on the family. Many parents have no idea what their children are watching because they're too involved with their own programs.

1   **How does the author feel about television?**

    A   He thinks television helps people discover their own interests.

    B   He thinks television isn't very good for family life.

    C   He thinks television is better than radio.

    D   He thinks television should not be watched after dinner.

The correct choice is **B**. The author believes that television has had a bad impact on the family because it reduces the amount of interaction between family members. The other choices are incorrect.

PURPOSE

Authors have a general purpose in mind when they write. They may want to teach or inform their readers, or to convince them to agree with them, or perhaps to amuse them.

Read the next example and decide on its author's purpose.

Example 2

It is always the poor who suffer when there are tax cuts. The rich will have more and the poor less. Tax cuts mean budget cutting. How can we in good conscience agree to this? I ask you to take a moment and look deep within yourself to find an answer. What will future generations say of such cruel policies?

     Why do you think the author wrote the lines printed above?

    A   to amuse readers with tax jokes

    B   to instruct readers on tax payments

    C   to persuade readers to oppose the tax cuts

    D   to inform readers about the budget

The author of this selection wanted to persuade readers that tax cuts were not a good idea. **Choice C** is correct.

Read the next selection and decide what the author's purpose is.

Example 3

Heat garlic in oil until lightly golden. Add diced tomatoes and heat for 20 minutes over a low heat until they are tender. Crumble tuna into smaller pieces and add to tomato sauce. Simmer just enough to warm the tuna through; you don't want to boil it. Transfer cooked spaghetti to serving bowl and mix in tuna, tomatoes, parsley, and salt and pepper.

3   **The author's purpose is to**

    A   explain how to cook spaghetti with tunafish

    B   inform someone about the different types of spaghetti

    C   discuss the best way to prepare tunafish

    D   persuade people to eat more spaghetti

Choice A is correct. The author's purpose is to explain how to cook spaghetti with tunafish. The author isn't informing you about the types of spaghetti and isn't discussing the best way to prepare tunafish. Nor does the selection persuade you to eat more spaghetti.

Authors use many ways to get their ideas across. The language they choose has an effect on their readers. It makes them feel a particular way.

Read Example 4. What is the mood of this poem? How does it make you feel? What words did the author use to make you feel that way?

Example 4

This poem is 2,000 years old. It is about an orphan girl who works all the time. Her new parents treat her badly.

The Orphan

To be an orphan,
To be fated to be an orphan,
How bitter is this lot!
When my father and mother were alive
I used to ride in a carriage
With four fine horses.
But when they both died,
My brother and sister-in-law
Made me work hard day and night.

4 **What is the tone of this poem?**

   A   sad and forlorn

   B   satisfied and happy

   C   friendly to everyone

   D   fear

 Your teacher will discuss your answer.

USING GRAPHIC ORGANIZERS TO DETERMINE THE AUTHOR'S VIEWPOINT

The **New York State English Language Arts Test** may ask you questions about the author's viewpoint by showing you a graphic organizer, and asking you to identify the detail which the author thinks is most important.

Read the next passage, study the graphic, and decide which supporting fact the author thinks is most important.

Example 5

There are many kinds of dogs. Some are small, some are huge. Some like to run outdoors. And others prefer to sit by the fire. But dogs have been man's best friend since prehistoric days. Dogs have performed many tasks. When herdsmen herd their cows and sheep, dogs keep the animals in place. Dogs have led the blind, tracked down lost people, and pulled sleds in the Arctic.

But their great contribution has been in hunting. They have hunted with people all over the world, sometimes tracking lions, or retrieving birds, or cornering wild boars, or chasing foxes. Without the aid of dogs, many huntsmen would not have survived to bring meat home to their families.

5 You read that "dogs are man's best friend." How does the author try to convince readers that this statement is correct?

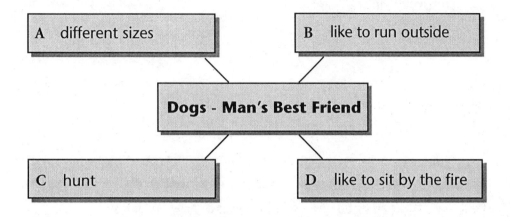

Choice C is correct. The other choices are in the passage, but they do not convince the reader that dogs are man's best friend.

PERSUASIVE DEVICES

Many writers want to persuade their readers to agree with them. The different techniques they use are called persuasive devices.

Decide what persuasive techniques the author is using in this letter to a local newspaper.

Example 6

To the Editor:

When children go out to play in the winter, they often like to eat snow and ice. Licking icicles and chewing snow may seem like harmless fun. But actually this seemingly innocent behavior can be quite dangerous.

Snow often contains lead. Lead is poisonous and especially dangerous to growing children. Lead in the snow comes from gasoline. Some older cars use gasoline which contains lead. When gasoline is burned in the engine, a gas is formed. If the gas contains lead, the lead eventually drops down into the snow on the ground. Even a little bit of lead is very dangerous. Lead can damage the brain as well as make a child sick.

Icicles are also dangerous. They often contain lead, too. Icicles are formed by the water that runs off the roof and freezes. If there is lead in the roofing material, it can go into the icicles, for this reason, most icicles that hang from roofs contain lead. Children like to break icicles off and then suck on them. They may think it is fun, but they are harming themselves.

More people should be aware of the danger of eating ice and snow. This would help keep children from getting lead poisoning.

Ruth Silverman

6   **The author of this letter tries to persuade her readers by**

    A   discussing the kinds of icicles there are

    B   appealing to people to keep their houses free of icicles

    C   stating the ways in which snow and ice can ruin a roof

    D   listing the reasons why snow and icicles are dangerous

The correct choice is **D**. The author of this letter lists the reasons why snow and icicles are dangerous. The other choices are incorrect.

STRATEGIES AND TIPS FOR IDENTIFYING THE AUTHOR'S VIEWPOINT AND PURPOSE

1.   Check for words and phrases that indicate how the author feels about a topic.

2.   The main reason authors write nonfictional passages is to *inform*. They may also hope to *instruct*, *persuade*, or *entertain* their readers.

3.   Where you read a selection can provide an important clue as to an author's purpose. Newspaper editorials are usually intended to persuade. School texts are intended to instruct.

4.   It may help if you know who the author is. Humorous writers, for example, probably want to amuse and entertain you.

5.   As you read, watch out for any persuasive devices the author has used.

    To analyze an editorial:

      •   decide on the main point the writer is making.

      •   pay attention to the details used to support this point.

      •   distinguish between the details that support this point, the details that support it poorly, and the details that don't support it at all.

SELECTIONS FOR PRACTICE

Selection 1

Dear Editor:

I went to the city zoo yesterday and I was horrified to see the way the animals there are treated. They are forced into caged-off areas that are far too small for their needs. In particular, I was offended by the quarters for the black bear. He barely has enough room to stretch out in his cage. Worse still, the people who were watching him were ignoring the "Don't Feed the Animals" sign. They were giving him junk food full of sugar and salt, which is very bad for his diet. I think it's time that the public spoke up. Either we must improve the zoo or we must close it and allow its animals to go to a facility that is more humane.

Sincerely,

Carolyn Short

1A **The author seems to think that**

   A   all zoos should be closed

   B   the local zoo should be improved

   C   the local zoo doesn't have enough animals

   D   animals should not be put on display

1B **What is the purpose of this letter?**

   A   to explain why zoos exist

   B   to inform the public about a bad situation

   C   to make fun of the animals in the zoo

   D   to discourage anyone from going to the zoo

Selection 2

Inventor's Magazine is read by people who invent new things. Once the magazine asked all their readers to vote on what they thought were the greatest inventions in the last 200 years.

What invention do you think came first? It was the safety pin. It seems such a simple idea, yet, until recently, millions of safety pins were needed every year just for baby diapers.

The invention which came in second was even simpler than the safety pin. It was the pencil with an eraser on top. Pencils never used to have an eraser attached. Someone thought of it one day and got rich.

Some inventions on the list, like the copying machine, were very complicated. However, a little more than half of the greatest inventions were things anyone could think of.

2 **The author's purpose in this selection is**

   A   to persuade the audience to read *Inventor's Magazine* every month

   B   to argue against choosing the safety pin as the greatest invention

   C   to make fun of inventors and their inventions

   D   to show how great inventions can be very simple

Selection 3

Nancy was late again. I stood outside the restaurant fuming. I should have realized that she could never be on time. It was already one o'clock, and we had agreed to eat at 12:30. I had to be back at work by 1:30. Sometimes I feel she only thinks about herself. Yet when I was in the hospital she visited me everyday, typed up her notes from class, and got everybody to come for my birthday party in the hospital.

My cousin Bob is a little like Mary. I can't figure him out. Some days he'll do anything for me and some days he doesn't seem to know I'm alive.

3 **The author shows that**

   A   most people can't be trusted

   B   people can be a mixture of good and bad

   C   waiting for people makes you angry

   D   it's better not to trust anyone

Selection 4

Bristlecone pines are remarkable. They are the longest-lived form of plant life in the world. These trees can live as long as 5,000 years. Some bristlecone pines standing today in the western United States were seedlings when the Egyptian pyramids were being built. They were mature trees by the year 1 AD. Bristlecone pines grow in only six western states. In an effort to preserve these ancient trees, the areas in which they grow have been incorporated into state parks. One of these areas, in eastern California, is called the Ancient Bristlecone Pine Forest. It contains some of the oldest and largest specimens.

Bristlecone pines grow on mountain tops or in remote places. They were unknown to the general public until a few decades ago, when a tree expert named Edmund Schulman wrote a widely-read magazine article about them. Ever since, people have traveled to the West to admire the age and beauty of these trees.

4   **According to the author, why are Bristlecone pines remarkable?**

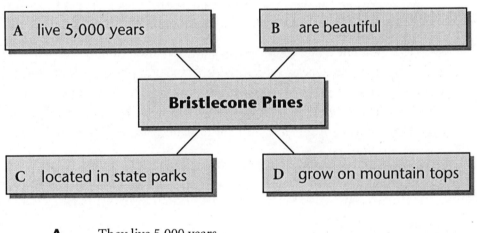

| A   live 5,000 years | B   are beautiful |

Bristlecone Pines

| C   located in state parks | D   grow on mountain tops |

    A   They live 5,000 years.

    B   They are beautiful.

    C   They are located in state parks.

    D   They grow on mountain tops.

Selection 5

Emiliano Zapata and Francisco Villa, known as Pancho Villa, were two of the leaders of the Mexican Revolution that began in 1910. A poor Indian villager from southern Mexico, Zapata wished to seize the land held by the rich landowners and give it to his people. Zapata organized and led an army of Indian farmers like himself. On three occasions, his army occupied Mexico City. But the governments Zapata helped to install never accomplished the land reforms that he advocated.

His fellow revolutionary, Pancho Villa, fought in the north. On one occasion, his army joined Zapata's army in occupying Mexico City. But, unlike Zapata, Villa was a bandit as well as a patriot. Sometimes he fought against injustice, and sometimes he just plain robbed people. In 1916, angered that the United States supported one of his rivals, he invaded the United States and killed 16 Americans. U.S. troops chased him back into Mexico, but failed to catch him.

5 **Why do you think the author includes the following sentence in describing Pancho Villa: "Sometimes he fought against injustice, and sometimes he just plain robbed people"?**

A   to emphasize what a great man Villa was

B   to indicate how lawless Mexico was in those days

C   to suggest that Villa was mentally ill

D   to underline the contrast between Zapata and Villa

9. UNDERSTANDING FIGURATIVE (NONLITERAL) LANGUAGE

Writers, especially poets, often achieve their effects by using language in a particular way. When writers use words and phrases in an unusual, nonliteral fashion, we say that they are using **figurative** language.

Read Example 1 and observe the language the author uses to describe the air.

Example 1

> The weather changed. The air had come down like a stagnant sea, weighing us down with its heavy pressure. Then, just as quickly, it lifted, like a rising cloud free of the restraints that held it to earth.

In this selection, the writer compares the air to a stagnant sea. Instead of saying the air was heavy, the writer uses figurative language to get our attention.

Read the passage again and then answer the question.

1 **When you read that the air lifted "like a rising cloud free of the restraints that held it to earth" you can guess that the air was becoming**

    A   unbearable

    B   heavier

    C   lighter

    D   threatening

Choice C is correct. The author compares the air to a rising cloud. This suggests that the air was getting lighter.

The next selection you will read is a poem. Sometimes poems are hard to understand because of their figurative language. They may require rereading.

Read this poem by the famous American poet Emily Dickinson as many times as you need to and then decide what it means.

Example 2

The Morns Are Meeker
by Emily Dickinson

The morns are meeker than they were,
The nuts are getting brown;
The berry's cheek is plumper,
The rose is out of town.

The maple wears a gayer scarf,
The field a scarlet gown.
Lest I should be old-fashioned,
I'll put a trinket on.

2 **What is the poet talking about when she says, "The maple wears a gayer scarf?"**

    A   Someone has wrapped a brightly-colored scarf around the maple tree.

    B   The leaves on the maple tree have changed to more brilliant colors.

    C   The maple tree is the only tree that has leaves.

    D   The maple tree is old and dying.

 Your teacher will discuss your answer.

STRATEGIES AND TIPS
FOR UNDERSTANDING FIGURATIVE LANGUAGE

1. The term, *figurative language*, means using words and phrases in an unusual way where they don't mean literally what they say.

2. Authors use figurative language to give their writing more color and power.

3. Most times, you can use context clues to understand what the author means.

4. Often, you need to read the whole passage or poem to understand words that are used figuratively.

SELECTIONS FOR PRACTICE

Selection 1

Touching her baby for the first time, she felt the downy surface that seemed to slide beneath her fingers like smoothest silk.

1   **Why would you guess the writer talks about "downy surface" resembling the "smoothest silk"?**

A   The mother is petting a silky, long-haired cat.

B   The baby is wearing a robe made of silky satin.

C   The baby's skin feels very soft.

D   The baby is having a bath and the water feels smooth.

Selection 2

A man glanced briefly at the poet and this glance has had a powerful impact upon her. It has left her feeling very uncertain.

Encounter
by Ellen D'Elia

It was only a small glance
But it stayed with me the whole day.
A moment in time that endured
More than I could foretell.
Peering within my quiet place,
He broke the silence of this dream,
And left instead an unknown doubt,
A questioning thought that never goes.

2A **This poem uses figurative language to describe a meeting with someone. What is the poet talking about when she uses the phrase "my quiet place"?**

    A   a place in the next town

    B   her inner thoughts

    C   the time of day

    D   the room in which she studies

2B **What do you think the poet is talking about?**

    A   How important it is that people not stare at each other.

    B   How much she dislikes the person she met

    C   How, sometimes, no one should speak

    D   How deeply she was affected by someone she saw

Selection 3

The ocean looked like some flattened wheat land. We stood on the edge of the beach, a browned desert that offered no safe refuge, and watched the faltering ship begin to fall helplessly into the sea.

3   **When the author describes the beach as a "browned desert," she means that**

A   it was foggy

B   it was filled with sand that drifted into the ocean

C   it looked barren and uninviting

D   it was filled with saltwater pools

PART 2: WRITING AND LISTENING

10. WRITING

The **New York State English Language Arts Test** will ask you to write some of your answers. When you do, be sure to use correct **punctuation**, **usage**, and **spelling**. Whenever you see the symbol below, be sure to plan and check your writing.

PUNCTUATION

END MARKS

End marks are the punctuation that goes at the end of a sentence. There are three common end marks:

(.)   the period, used after most statements and also after abbreviations.

(!)   the exclamation point, used after commands or statements that show excitement or strong emotion.

(?)   the question mark, used for questions.

Example 1

1   **Which sentence has the correct punctuation?**

  A   We can go to the zoo, but not to the beach

  B   Who will play the guitar at the party.

  C   Watch out for the hole!

  D   How did you do on the exam.

 Your teacher will discuss your answer.

COMMAS

Commas are used—

- to separate three or more items in a list:

    We need some cheese, meat, a loaf of bread, mustard, juice, and something for dessert.

- to separate two or more words describing a word that follows:

    It was a long, hard, dangerous hike.

- after introductory clauses beginning with words like *if, when, because, after, before,* etc.:

    After we got to the visitor's center, they told us it was too late to enter.

- after two or more introductory phrases:

    On the morning of May 1, we are holding a brunch for Rashan.

Commas are also used to separate two independent clauses joined by the words *and, but, or, nor, for,* and *yet*:

Commas should **NOT** be used to separate two verbs sharing the same subject and joined by the word *and*:

WRONG:	Greenwich Village in New York City is a tourist attraction, and is a place where many artists and writers live. (The two verbs are both *is*. The subject of both is Greenwich Village.)
CORRECT:	Greenwich Village in New York City is a tourist attraction and is a place where many artists and writers live. (no comma after *attraction*.)

And commas should NOT be used to separate only two items in a list.

WRONG:	I'm going to buy coffee, and tea.
CORRECT:	I'm going to buy coffee and tea. (no comma after coffee.)

Example 2

2   **Which sentence does not use the comma correctly?**

A   Senegal, and Sierra Leone are located on the west coast of Africa.

B   Senegalese food draws from native, French, Arabic, and Portuguese traditions.

C   When Muslims observe the holy month of Ramadan, they must fast from sunrise to sunset for the entire month.

D   Visiting Senegal is a fascinating, enjoyable, memorable experience.

 Your teacher will discuss your answer.

APOSTROPHES

Apostrophes are used:

- To take the place of missing letters or numbers

    They're going on a trip to Europe next month. (They are going on a trip to Europe next month.)

    I graduated from high school in '85. (I graduated from high school in 1985.)

- To show possession

    George Washington's wife was named Martha.

The last example shows possession by one person or thing. To show possession by more than one person, you add only an apostrophe if the plural word already ends in *s*:

    The teachers' books were in the closet.

When a plural word does not end in s, you show possession by adding *'s*.

    Children's toys are on sale.

SPECIAL RULE! OFTEN TESTED!

- The word *it's* (with an apostrophe) means "it is." For example:

    It's not likely I will travel to Tibet.

- The word *its* (NO apostrophe) means "belonging to it." For example:

    The raccoon washed its food before eating it.

Example 3

3	Which sentence does not use the apostrophe correctly?

A   The alligator's mouth snapped tight.

B   You could hear it's humming all night long.

C   The women's cars were parked behind the bank.

D   Most of the boys' bats were made of wood.

Choice B does not use the apostrophe correctly. It's should be replaced by *its*, the possessive. In the other three sentences, the apostrophe is used correctly.

CAPITALIZATION

- The first word in a sentence is always capitalized.

    One place is as good as the other for a picnic.

- The titles of movies, plays, and books also begin with capitals:

    The Titanic

    Romeo and Juliet

- All words in titles are also capitalized except short words, such as the articles *a, an, the*; the short conjunctions *and, but, or, for*; and the short prepositions like *in, from, to, into*:

    Where the Red Fern Grows

    The Last of the Mohicans

    "The Yellow Rose of Texas"

    "America the Beautiful"

- Proper nouns (names, companies, places, and holidays, for example) are always capitalized. In place names like Atlantic Ocean or Amazon River, both parts of the name are capitalized:

    Saugerties observes Memorial Day with a parade through the center of town.

- Titles such as mayor, principal, aunt, and congressman, are capitalized when they appear before a name. Titles are not usually capitalized when they follow a name or are used without a name, unless they belong to a high office holder.

    Aunt Ellen prefers to be called Professor Kimbell.

    The President spoke to the senators about the judges' ruling.

Example 4

4   **Which sentence does not use capitalization correctly?**

A   The head of the department said that all employees must take a refresher course at Niagara Community College.

B   The Museum of Fine Arts will have a special Monet show in September.

C   Some businesses, like business and personal computers, inc., will participate in the fundraiser.

D   Uncle Charles served in World War II.

Choice C does not use capitalization correctly. In this sentence, "business and personal computers, inc." is a company name and should be capitalized.

USAGE

SUBJECT-VERB AGREEMENT

When you write a sentence, it is important to make sure that the verb agrees with the subject. Before you can do this, you must know whether that subject is singular (one person or thing) or plural (more than one person or thing).

In the sentence—

The doctor treats children.

—the word *doctor* is singular. Note how the verb changes when there is more than one doctor:

The doctors treat children.

Example 5

5   **In which sentence does the verb not agree with the subject?**

A   Mr. Boris owns a dress shop.

B   Barry wants to volunteer with Habitat.

C   The clowns come into the tent with the horses.

D   Christina get a new dress for the party.

Choice D shows incorrect usage. "Christina" is the subject of this sentence and is singular. The sentence should read: "Christina gets a new dress for the party."

PRONOUNS

Sometimes we use pronouns in the place of nouns. The following pronouns are always singular:

I	He	She	It
One	Each	Everybody	Everyone
Everything	None	Nobody	Nothing

Here is a list of personal pronouns:

Subject	**Object**
I	me
you	you
he, she, it	him, her, it
we	us
you	you
they	them

The sentences below show you how these pronouns are used.

She seems to know all the answers.

They became good at chess.

May she and I come to the movie too?

Give the present to us right now!

Ricardo handed a book to her and me. (**NOT "her and I"!**)

Neither he nor I will join the club.

Veronica asked Beverly and me to watch her swim in the competition.
(**NOT "Beverly and I"!**)

There's a simple test for this last kind of sentence. Try it without the word *Beverly*:

Veronica asked me to watch her swim in the competition.

Veronica asked I to watch her swim in the competition.

The first is clearly correct. So we say:

Veronica asked Beverly and me to watch her swim in the competition.
(**NOT "Beverly and I"!**)

Example 6

6   In which sentence are the pronouns used correctly?

   A   Him and me are the best spellers in the class.

   B   The teacher gave a test to her and me.

   C   She and me have been going to ballet lessons for years.

   D   I thought Ted had gone to the play with they.

Choice B is correct. Object pronouns are used after prepositions like *to, from, with*. So "her and me" is correct and "she and I" incorrect.

SPELLING

You can improve your spelling by using a dictionary, learning words your teacher gives you, and, most of all, by reading. The more you read, the more words you will see spelled correctly.

Many words sound the same or similar but are spelled differently. Here you can see how some of these word pairs are used:

We will **accept** your kind offer.

They brought everything **except** their keys.

I need **advice** on this problem.

I **advise** you to ask for extra help.

Lack of sleep can **affect** how you feel.

The **effect** of war on the people was terrible.

This **brake** needs repair.

Don't **break** those expensive glasses!

Albany is the **capital** of New York.

The state assembly is in the **capitol** building.

Burlap is a **coarse** cloth.

The golf **course** was crowded on Saturday.

The city **council** meets today.

Her **counsel** helped us decide what to do.

He rode a camel across the **desert**.

The best **dessert** was the carrot cake.

The children said the rule wasn't **fair**.

Did you pay your bus **fare**?

In court, we behave **formally**.

Formerly, she was a teacher's aide.

I **hear** they are now engaged.

Here are the most recent facts and figures.

It's a large, striped, female cat.

Its owner worried too much about the cat.

Napoleon **led** his army to victory.

The pencil **lead** broke in my hand.

The pants were too **loose** on him.

I **lose** keys and umbrellas frequently.

Go **past** the school and turn left.

Time **passed** and she recovered.

We hope for a lasting **peace**.

I lost a **piece** of that puzzle.

The horse galloped over the **plain**.

The **plane** flew off into the clouds.

The **principal** made a new rule.

We learned a new **principle** in math.

You can't move the **stationary** desks.

His **stationery** had his name on it.

Better late **than** never.

Then the pot began to boil over.

Their ideas are interesting.

There is nothing happening here.

The pitcher **threw** the ball.

The ball went **through** the window.

You don't want to **waste** it, do you?

Around his **waist** was a leather belt.

The **weather** has been rotten.

I don't know **whether** or not it is true.

QUESTIONS FOR PRACTICE

1   **Which sentence is punctuated correctly?**

A   "Get back"! the policeman shouted as he moved the crowd to the side of the street.

B   The painter finished the child's portrait.

C   Its sad that we don't see our cousins more often.

D   "When can I leave for the mall"? asked Jennifer.

2   **Which sentence does not use the comma correctly?**

A   The Santanas like to spend time in town, and in the country.

B   They enjoy skiing, sledding, and skating in the winter.

C   The family grows vegetables and herbs in its garden in the summer.

D   Because Dr. Santana works at home, the family is free to go to the country whenever they want when school isn't in session.

3   **Which sentence does not use the apostrophe correctly?**

A   The bird's beak was very sharp.

B   The cat pounced on it's prey.

C   The women's whispers couldn't be heard over the fan.

D   Three of the boys' uniforms were torn.

4   **Which sentence does not use capitalization correctly?**

A   My favorite trip is to the Museum of Natural History in New York City.

B   The buffalo bills are having a great season.

C   Carrie went to a dance on New Year's Eve.

D   The Longworth Company is located on Washington Avenue.

5   **In which sentence does the verb not agree with the subject?**

A   Mr. Hernandez owns a grocery store.

B   Chuck wants to volunteer to do the clean-up.

C   The nurses arrive at seven in the morning.

D   Ginnie get to the door before the cat.

6   **In which sentence are the pronouns used correctly?**

A   Her and me went to the grocery store to buy candy.

B   Coach gave letters to him and me.

C   He and me aren't going to go to the workshop.

D   I never thought you would go to the game with they.

7   **Read the sentences and decide which words are spelled incorrectly.**
If all the words in a sentence are spelled correctly, choose D,
No mistake.

1   <u>Whose</u> making <u>dessert</u> for the <u>dinner</u> Wednesday? <u>No mistake</u>.
    A   B   C   D

2   <u>There</u> are <u>two</u> misspelled words on that <u>piece</u> of paper. <u>No mistake</u>.
    A   B   C   D

3   You will <u>recieve</u> your free gift in the <u>mail</u> <u>Tuesday</u>. <u>No mistake</u>.
         A   B   C   D

4   The <u>weather</u> in New York in <u>February</u> can <u>be</u> freezing. <u>No mistake</u>.
       A   B   C   D

5   The puppy didn't <u>know</u> <u>it's</u> name or <u>where</u> it lived. <u>No mistake</u>.
            A B   C   D

6   The <u>principal</u> asked <u>whether</u> I <u>prefered</u> French or Spanish. <u>No mistake</u>.
     A   B   C   D

11. WRITING STRATEGIES

This part of *The Coach* will give you more practice in writing your answers.

Here are some good rules to follow.

USING DETAILS FROM THE PASSAGE

Many questions ask you to include details from the selection.

Read the selection about Henry and Agnes.

Example 1

Agnes fell in love with Henry when they were seniors in high school. Agnes played in the school orchestra and Henry was a member of the choir. Often Henry sang solos at performances. Agnes loved to listen to Henry's voice. She would sit in her chair holding her violin and hum to the songs that he sang. She thought he had the finest tenor voice she had ever heard. She especially loved it when he sang Irish melodies. The sound of his voice brought tears to her eyes. After they were married and had a family, Agnes always told their children she fell in love with their father not just because he was a wonderful person but also because of his voice.

1A **Discuss what Agnes thought about Henry.**

Victor's answer:

Agnes loved Henry because he could sing.

Sean's answer:

Agnes fell in love with Henry in high school. She loved listening to him sing, especially Irish songs. His songs made her cry. After their marriage she told their children that one reason she fell in love was because of Henry's beautiful voice.

Mike's answer:

Agnes said that she fell in love with Henry. Singing is a good way to meet people especially if you like music. I like music a lot but I don't think I could fall in love with someone because of music. But my sister likes music and she likes to sing. She likes all kinds of music.

1B **Which person answered the question appropriately using details from the story?**

A Victor

B Sean

C Mike

  Your teacher will discuss your answer.

STAY ON TARGET

When you answer questions on the **New York State English Language Arts Test**, it is important to stay on target. If the question asks if you like baseball, write about that. Don't write about computers. Stick to the topic.

Read the story and then read Christina's and Nina's answers. Decide who stayed on target.

Example 2

The grizzly bear, one of the largest bears in the world, can be a terrifying sight. When it stands erect, it can reach nine feet and weigh over 1,000 pounds. I doubt that there's any human being that would care to tackle an angry grizzly.

This bear is omnivorous in its eating habits. It consumes fish, berries, meat, and fruit. But the biggest treat of all for a grizzly is honey. Grizzly bears like honey so much that if a grizzly finds an old log with a bees' nest, it will rip the wood away with its powerful claw and eat the honey. Grizzlies have long thick fur to protect their skin so they can just ignore bee stings.

Grizzly bears spend the year eating and getting fat. Then in the winter they find a warm cave in a quiet part of the woods and doze through the winter months. The grizzly doesn't eat during the winter, living instead on the fat it stored the remainder of the year.

2A **How do grizzlies feel about honey?**

Christina's answer:

Grizzlies love honey. It's a treat for them. They like it so much that they will rip apart a log to get at a bees' nest. They don't even stop if the bees sting them. They have thick fur that protects them.

Nina's answer:

Honey is very good for you. It is sold in health food stores all through New York State. It's not very fattening unless you eat a lot. Some people can't eat honey because it makes them sick, but I love it.

2B **Which person stayed on target?**

  A   Christina

  B   Nina

 Your teacher will discuss your answer.

ANSWERING ALL PARTS OF THE QUESTION

Sometimes a question will ask which you like the best—baseball or basketball. You can't just write about baseball and forget about basketball. You have to talk about both baseball and basketball.

Read the selection and the question. Then decide whether Leigh Ann answered all parts of the question.

Example 3

Ever since Tawana was a child, she knew she wanted to be a nurse. She enjoyed helping people who were sick. She had great patience and kind words for all. The other health professionals she worked with praised her skills and her ability to motivate sick people to get well. Her sister Deedee wasn't that way at all. She couldn't stand hospitals or medicine. She didn't like to take care of anyone. She wouldn't have a pet because she didn't want to have to feed it and care for it. She lived alone.

3A   **What did Tawana and her sister think of taking care of others?**

Leigh Ann's answer:

Tawana knew she wanted to be a nurse when she was a child. She enjoyed helping sick people. She was patient and was praised for her skills. She could get people to want to get well.

3B **What's wrong with Leigh Ann's answer?**

  A   She didn't give any examples.

  B   She gave too much information about Tawana.

  C   She didn't talk about Deedee.

  D   She didn't stay on target.

The correct choice is **C**. Leigh Ann was asked about Tawana and her sister Deedee, but her answer just discussed Tawana.

Now you will read a longer selection.

SELECTION FOR PRACTICE

Selection 1

Sam loved to sit on Jimmy's shoulder. He also loved to take little showers in the sink. Sam sang in the morning and the evening, and he flew in circles in his room. But Sam wasn't always this way.

When Jimmy first saw Sam, he was in a cage in a dark corner of a pet store. He didn't look very happy. The store was going out of business and Sam was on sale. Jimmy's mom and dad decided a bird would make a good pet, so they brought him home. Sam had a nice new cage, much bigger than his old one. And he could look out the window and see birds and squirrels and trees and bushes. But Sam was very quiet. He never made a sound.

Still, Jimmy would sit by the cage and talk to Sam. He whistled to him and made bird sounds. He brought Sam special food and talked quietly to him. One night he dreamed that Sam jumped on his shoulder and sang softly in his ear. It made Jimmy feel very happy.

Jimmy and his family went away on a trip. Sam was left in his cage under the care of a friend who came once a day to change his water and make sure he had enough to eat.

When Jimmy got back, he opened the door of the cage. All of a sudden Sam flew onto his hand. Jimmy couldn't believe it. Then he started to sing a wonderful song. From then on Sam was Jimmy's best friend. He would always sit on his shoulder when Jimmy was working on his homework. He would eat out of Jimmy's hand and walk on his head. Jimmy loved his pet bird very much.

One day, Jimmy's mother opened the door to go into the backyard. She had forgotten Sam was out of his cage. Sam flew to the door and sailed out into the yard. For a moment, he stayed in a nearby tree; then he just flew off and no one ever saw him again. But Jimmy never forgot him.

1A The story says that at first Sam never made a sound. How did Jimmy react to this? What happened? Give examples from the story.

Pauline's answer:

At first Sam was very quiet. But then Jimmy talked to him and brought special food to him and whistled to him. Jimmy had a dream that Sam jumped on his shoulder. And it came true. After Jimmy came back from a trip, Sam flew on his hand and he sang to him, and he ate out of Jimmy's hand.

Answer these questions.

	No	Yes
Did Pauline answer all the questions?	( )	( )
Did Pauline stay on target?	( )	( )
Did Pauline give examples from the story?	( )	( )

Most students answer these three questions with "Yes." Pauline answered all the questions, stayed on target, and gave examples from the story.

STRATEGIES AND TIPS
FOR WRITING ANSWERS TO QUESTIONS

Be sure that:
- you answer the question that is asked
- you answer all parts of the question
- you include details and examples from the story
- you stay on target

Be sure that you do NOT:
- answer with just one or two words

Now you will write your own answer to Number 1B. You can reread the story as much as you want to before you write your answer.

1B The story says that Sam was Jimmy's best friend. Why does the author say this? Give examples from the story in your answer. (You can look back at the story or at Pauline's answer to help you write your own answer. You can also write notes in the space below.)

Notes

_____

_____

_____

_____

_____

_____

_____

Your Answer

_____

_____

_____

_____

_____

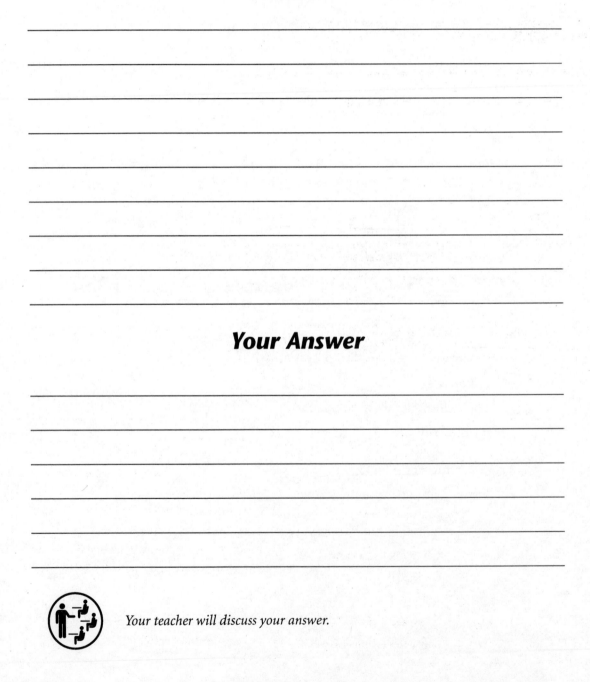

Your teacher will discuss your answer.

12. APPLYING YOUR WRITING SKILLS

WRITING SHORT AND LONG RESPONSES

Sometimes the questions on the **New York State English Language Arts Test** ask you to write short answers and sometimes long answers.

You can tell if an answer is short or long by the number of lines. For a short answer, there will only be six lines. If the answer is long, there will be many more lines.

When you write a long answer, you will see this sign:

This means you will be graded on your spelling, punctuation, capitalization, and grammar.

The next selection will give you a chance to practice your writing skills.

Selection 1

Few children know that the traditional picture of Santa Claus as a plump, white-bearded old man in a fur-trimmed red suit was the invention of an American cartoonist named Thomas Nast. Nast created this image of Santa Claus over a hundred years ago and it has stayed the same ever since. Nast also gave our major political parties their well-known animal symbols: he popularized the Democratic donkey and created the Republican elephant. He also originated the image of Uncle Sam, the symbol of the United States, with his top hat and striped pants.

Image making was Thomas Nast's profession. For about thirty-five years, from the Civil War to the late 1890s, he was the most famous and powerful political cartoonist in America. He is most widely known for his cartoon campaign against "Boss" Tweed. Tweed was a New York City politician who made a huge personal fortune by taking bribes and by adding extra costs to government building projects and then keeping that money for himself. Tweed cost New York City millions of dollars.

Thomas Nast was born in Germany and came to this country with his mother when he was six. At an early age, Nast showed a great talent for drawing. By the time he was 15, he had already started to work as an artist for a weekly magazine. While working there, he met many of the leading artists of the day, who gave him advice and help.

At the age of 20, he traveled to Europe to draw pictures of news events that were happening there. He went to England and then to Italy to cover a revolt. However, when the Civil War broke out, he hurried back to the United States. During the war, he drew pictures of soldiers in training camps. He also started to draw political cartoons. Nast vigorously supported the war and was opposed to slavery. President Abraham Lincoln called Nast "our best recruiting sergeant" because of his cartoons making fun of Northerners who opposed the war, and because his cartoons showed the evils of slavery and the benefits of freedom.

Even after the Civil War, Nast continued to draw pictures that were political in nature. He joined the staff of a famous magazine, Harper's Weekly, and drew cartoons about everything important that was happening.

In 1869, Nast decided to use his cartoons to expose Tweed's "misdeeds." Nast hated dishonesty and so he drew many cartoons that showed what Tweed and the "Tweed Ring"—the name Tweed's supporters were given—were up to. In one of his most famous cartoons, he created a caricature of Tweed, a distorted image that indicated how greedy he was, showing him with small beady eyes and a huge, fat body. Nast used his cartoons to tell the public about Tweed's crimes.

These drawings had a powerful effect on public opinion; soon everyone knew about Tweed's corruption. Tweed became so frightened of Nast that he tried to bribe him to stop drawing the cartoons. When that failed, he tried harassment. He threatened Nast's life and tried to keep magazines from publishing his cartoons. Nast never gave up, and eventually, Tweed was put in jail.

Because of Nast's cartoons, his face was known all over the world. Tweed escaped from jail and fled to Spain. The Spanish police recognized him and he was again arrested. He was returned to the United States and placed in prison once more. When Tweed died in jail in 1878, it was discovered that he owned every single one of the Boss Tweed cartoons Nast had created.

Late in his life, Nast stopped producing cartoons. He also lost most of his money. President Theodore Roosevelt appointed Nast as consul general of Guayaquil, Ecuador, in 1902. But soon after he took up his duties, he became ill and died.

During his life, Nast was a painter and book illustrator as well as a cartoonist. However, he will always be mostly remembered for his cartoons.

Now write a short answer to this question.

1   **Why did President Lincoln say Nast was our "best recruiting sergeant"?**

Explain your answer using details from the article.

_____

_____

_____

_____

_____

 Your teacher will discuss your answer

Planning Page

The next question asks for a long answer.

You may use this page to plan your answer to question 2.

2 You read that Nast did many cartoons of "Boss Tweed." What effect did his cartoons have on Boss Tweed? Use details from the story.

 Check your writing for correct spelling, grammar, capitalization, and punctuation.

_____

_____

_____

_____

_____

_____

_____

_____

_____

_____

_____

_____

_____

_____

 Your teacher will discuss your answer.

WRITING ANSWERS ANALYZING CHARACTER

3 Complete the chart with words or phrases that describe Thomas Nast's character. Then identify information from the article that supports each character trait.

Character Trait	Supporting Information
1. _____	_____
2. _____	_____
3. _____	_____

 Your teacher will discuss your answer.

WRITING ANSWERS COMPARING CHARACTERS

4 Compare Thomas Nast and Boss Tweed. How were they alike? How were they different? Use examples in your answers.

Thomas Nast

_____

_____

_____

_____

_____

_____

Boss Tweed

_____

_____

_____

_____

_____

_____

 Your teacher will discuss your answers.

WRITING ANSWERS BASED ON TWO SELECTIONS

Some questions will ask you to write an answer based on two selections rather than one selection. Try to find ideas that are similar or different in Selection 2 and Selection 3. Then answer question 5.

Selection 2

    Jaime Escalante taught math in a public school in East Los Angeles. He cared for his students and taught them well. He achieved national fame when his students outperformed students from elite private schools on a calculus exam.

Jaime Escalante grew up in La Paz, Bolivia. Later he moved to the United States, where he taught math at Garfield High School in Los Angeles. Garfield was a zoo. A gentle principal had allowed gangs to take over control of the school.

Escalante worked things out his own way. First off, he invited every able-bodied student to help him to scrape the graffiti off the desks and repaint the classroom. Then he began using whatever techniques he could to motivate his students. He challenged them to a game of handball: "You beat me, you get an A. If you don't beat me, you do this homework." Escalante always won.

Escalante knew the students were in gangs. He learned their gang names. He pretended to take the thumbprints of those in trouble with the police. He told them this way he'd find out if they were the graffiti experts messing up school books. Or he'd try bribery. Little pieces of candy would be handed out on test days. Patting shoulders, he'd whisper: "Don't be afraid of the test . . . should be sweet." His students had to work. He would make the work fun, but they had to do their part. No excuses. No absence slips. No dropping out.

A student who had been out for two days asked for a slip. Escalante replied: "Okay, okay. Here's one. Fill in your name. Thank you. That will be ten cents." The student protested and Escalante replied, "You're right. That's very unprofessional of me. Instead, why don't you just tell me why you didn't come to school the last two days, and I no charge you anything."

To help his calculus students understand inequalities, he had the class discuss the relative heights of LA Lakers Norm Nixon and Kareem Abdul-Jabbar. The kids hated factoring. So Escalante used a model of Charlie Brown with moving jaws that mouthed, "factoring, factoring." It was silly. It didn't mean a thing. But factoring was now a joke they couldn't forget. He couldn't remember students' names. On bad days they were all "burros" (mules). Those who skipped their homework were told: "Take off. It's time to fly." But guidance counselors were in league with Escalante. Playing good cop to Escalante's bad cop, they begged him to take the student back.

Selection 3

This poet wrote about American pioneers.

We are the builders,
The builders of tomorrow,
With lightness in our step and
    intentness in our eye.
And let us build tomorrow
Till it stand like a cathedral
With its stone foundation and its spires
    gleaming high.

We are the builders,
The builders of tomorrow.
It is not always easy.
We may stumble, or even fall.
But we look towards our goal.
Choosing the work we can do.
The few that are special will make the stained glass,
More of us will labor with the wood.
But all shall be the artisans,
And all shall build together,
Till the evening overtakes us and we know our work was good.

    —Adapted from "The Echo" by Elise Jane Jacobs, A Half-Century of
    Song, An Anthology of Hunter College Verse

Use this space to plan your answer to Number 5.

5 Jaime Escalante believed in the future of his students. The poet Elise Jacobs writes of building the future. Choose a line or lines from the poem. Discuss the meaning of your selection, and explain how it applies to Jaime Escalante.

Check your writing for correct spelling, grammar, and punctuation.

_____

_____

_____

_____

_____

_____

_____

_____

_____

_____

_____

_____

_____

_____

_____

 Your teacher will discuss your answer.

WRITING ANSWERS BASED ON THE AUTHOR'S PURPOSE

Some questions ask you to write an essay based on the purpose the author had for writing the article, essay, or poem. Decide what the author's purpose is by studying the language in the selection.

 6 Reread the poem "Pioneers." What is most likely the poet's purpose in writing this poem? Use ideas from the poem to support your answer.

 Your teacher will discuss your answer.

WRITING ANSWERS BASED ON YOUR KNOWLEDGE OR EXPERIENCE

Some questions will ask you to answer a question based on what you know, feel or have experienced. Pick a subject that you know well. Make sure to answer the whole question. Give reasons for your answer.

Use this space to plan your answer to Number 7.

7   Write an essay on someone in history or someone you know who
has achieved or helped someone else achieve a dream or fulfill an
ambition.

In your article, be sure to include:

- who the person is
- what he or she did
- the challenges that were overcome
- an introduction, a body, and a conclusion.

Check your writing for correct spelling, grammar, and
punctuation.

_____

_____

_____

_____

_____

_____

_____

_____

_____

_____

_____

_____

_____

_____

Your teacher will discuss your answer.

13. LISTENING

In the **English Language Arts Test** you will be asked to listen to selections and then answer questions about them. You will hear the selections twice. The first time you should listen carefully, but you cannot take notes. You will then hear the selection a second time. This time you should take notes. You should write down important details from the selection. You will need to remember many details to write your answers.

Example 1

This selection was written by General Ulysses S. Grant, who headed the Northern Army at the end of the Civil War. Grant had just received a letter of surrender from General Robert E. Lee, who headed the Confederate Army. Grant hated the fact that Lee believed in slavery, but he still respected Lee, who had been his major foe for many years. The passage is adapted from his autobiography.

> **TEACHER READS SELECTION FOR FIRST TIME.**

Now your teacher will read the selection again. This time take notes.

> **TEACHER READS THE SELECTION AGAIN. STUDENT CAN TAKE NOTES.**

General Ullysses S. Grant

General Robert E. Lee

Notes

1   General Grant says he did not feel happy at the defeat of Lee. Why did Grant feel sad? Include details from the passage in your answer.

_____

_____

_____

_____

_____

_____

 Your teacher will discuss your answer

NOTE TAKING

What did you write down? Did the notes you took help you answer the question? Your notes should include important details.

Many selections include a discussion of people. You may be asked to compare two people, as in the next example. Your notes should tell you how people are similar and how thay are different.

Example 2

This selection is about Private Sanders and Captain Hacker. As you listen, see if you can learn how these two men are similar and how they are different.

> **TEACHER READS SELECTION FOR FIRST TIME.**

Now your teacher will read the selection again. This time take notes.

> **TEACHER READS THE SELECTION AGAIN. STUDENT CAN TAKE NOTES.**

Notes

2A Using specific details from the passage, complete the chart below to show what each man was like.

Captain Hacker	Private Sanders

 Your teacher will discuss your answers

2B Why did Captain Hacker want to teach Private Sanders a lesson?
Use details from the selection.

_____

_____

_____

_____

_____

_____

_____

 Your teacher will discuss your answers

Example 3

Now your teacher will read you two letters. They are written by people who are visiting places that are new to them. The first one is entitled "A Letter from the Yukon." It was written by a person who had just moved to the Yukon. The Yukon is an area of Canada where it is very, very cold in the winter.

The second one is called "My First Trip to Puerto Rico." This letter was written by someone who visited her father's birthplace for the first time.

The first time your teacher reads the two passages, listen but don't take notes.

> **TEACHER READS "A LETTER FROM THE YUKON" AND "MY FIRST TRIP TO PUERTO RICO." STUDENT DOES NOT TAKE NOTES.**

The second time your teacher reads the two passages, take notes. You may use your notes to answer the questions that follow.

> **TEACHER READS "A LETTER FROM THE YUKON" AND "MY FIRST TRIP TO PUERTO RICO." STUDENT TAKES NOTES.**

Notes

Notes

3A How does the Yukon differ from Puerto Rico? In your answer you
may discuss living conditions, climate, language, or any other
subject mentioned in the letters. Use specific details to complete
the chart below.

The Yukon	**Puerto Rico**

3B Jenna says that in spite of hardships and a few scary moments, she and Tom love it in the Yukon. What hardships and scary moments does she mean? Use details from the letter to support your answer.

_____

_____

_____

_____

_____

_____

3C Why does Donna say that going to Ponce was the best part of the trip? Use details from the letter to support your answer.

_____

_____

_____

_____

_____

_____

Your teacher will discuss your answers

Planning Page

You may plan your writing for Number 3C here. But do not write your final answer on this page. Write your final answer beginning on the next page.

3D   **What new things do Jenna and Donna experience? Use details from their letters to support your answer.**

In your discussion, be sure to include

- **how their experiences compare to each other**
- **what they found different from their own home**
- **what they learned while they were visiting**

Check your writing for correct spelling, grammar, and punctuation.

_____

_____

_____

_____

_____

_____

_____

_____

_____

_____

_____

_____

_____

 Your teacher will discuss your answer.

Example 4

The next passages are about Native Americans. They are called "Buffie and Gene" and "Chief Osceola." The first is about two Mohawk Indians and the second about a Seminole chief named Osceola. The first time your teacher reads the two essays, listen but don't take notes.

> **TEACHER READS "BUFFIE AND GENE" AND "CHIEF OSCEOLA." STUDENT DOES NOT TAKE NOTES.**

The second time your teacher reads the essays take notes. You may use your notes to answer the questions below.

Here are some words and definitions you will need to know as you listen to the essays.

"Buffie and Gene"

    truce   cease fire

"Chief Osceola"

    reservation   federal land given to native Americans for their use

> **TEACHER READS "BUFFIE AND GENE" AND "CHIEF OSCEOLA" AGAIN. STUDENT TAKES NOTES.**

Notes

Notes

4A Using specific details from the passages, complete the chart below comparing Buffie to Gene.

Buffie and Gene

Similarities	Differences

4B How has life changed for Buffie and Gene? Give details from the selection.

_____

_____

_____

_____

_____

_____

_____

4C   **How has life changed for Gene in the last 40 years?**

_____

_____

_____

_____

_____

_____

4D   **The author says that Osceola would be proud of his great-grandchildren. Why is this true? Give details from the selection.**

_____

_____

_____

_____

_____

_____

 Your teacher will discuss your answers

Planning Page

You may plan your writing for Number 4D here. But do not write your final answer on this page. Write your final answer beginning on the next page.

4E Buffie and Gene faced changes in their lives. So did Chief Osceola. How were Buffie's and Gene's reactions different from Chief Osceola's?

Check your writing for correct spelling, grammar, and punctuation.

_____

_____

_____

_____

_____

_____

_____

_____

_____

_____

_____

_____

_____

_____

_____

Your teacher will discuss your answer.

PART 3: PRACTICE TEST

The test is divided into 2 "sessions:"

- **Session 1—Reading/Multiple Choice**. You will read three selections and answer multiple-choice questions about them.
  Listening/Writing. You will listen to a story and take notes. Then you will write your answers to some questions about the stories.

- **Session 2—Reading/Writing**. You will read some selections and write your answers to questions about them.

Read each selection carefully, including any definitions you may see at the bottom of the page. Then answer the questions about the selection. When you answer multiple-choice questions, circle the letter next to the answer you choose for each question. When you see the words GO ON at the bottom of a page, keep going. When you come to the word STOP at the bottom of the page, stop and put down your pencil.

TEST-TAKING TIPS

- Listen carefully to the directions. Be sure to read all of the directions in the Sample Test Guide. Ask your teacher to explain any directions you do not understand.

- Read or listen to each selection carefully. Read each question carefully. As you answer the questions, you may look back at the reading selections or your notes as often as you like.

- Plan your time. You may want to glance quickly through the entire session before you begin to answer questions in order to budget your time.

When you write your answers, be sure to include details from the reading or listening selection to support or explain your answer carefully and completely.

Your writing will NOT be scored on your personal opinions. It WILL be scored on:

- how clearly you organize and express your ideas

- how accurately and completely you answer the questions

- how well you support your ideas with examples

- how interesting and enjoyable your writing is

- how correctly you use grammar, spelling, punctuation, and paragraphs

You will be scored on your grammar, spelling, and punctuation only when you see this symbol.

The test is divided into Session 1 and Session 2.

Session 1

Directions

In this part of the test, you are going to read an article, a story, and a speech, and answer questions about what you have read. You may look back at the stories as often as you like. Circle the letter next to the answer you choose for each question.

When you see the words GO ON at the bottom of a page, keep going.

When you come to the word STOP at the bottom of the page, you have finished the first session.

Now begin.

Go On

Directions

This article discusses immigration. Read it and then do Numbers 1 through 8.

America's Immigrants

INDUSTRY IN THE UNITED STATES could not have expanded had there not been men, women, and children to work in the factories and mines of this growing country. Some of the new factory workers were farm workers who had been replaced by agricultural machinery. But mostly they came from abroad. The number of people living in the United States tripled between 1870 and 1920, largely as a result of immigration.

Immigrants to the United States	
Date	Place of Origin
Before 1720	England, Africa, Scotland
1720 – 1840	Britain, Germany, Africa, Ireland
1840 – 1860	Ireland, Germany, Britain
1860 – 1885	Germany, Britain, Ireland, Scandinavia, French-Canada
1885-1915	Italy, Poland, Russia, Greece, Czechoslovakia, Britain, Ireland, Germany, Armenia, China, Japan

The table shows the change in immigration patterns. The earliest immigrants came from Britain and (as slaves) from Africa. People forced to come from Africa played a major role in building our country. Germans came in large numbers after 1720, seeking land and jobs, and later, political freedom. In the 1840's, the Irish arrived, fleeing a land devastated by the failure of the potato crop, their main food.

After 1880, most immigrants were from southern and eastern Europe—Poles, Czechs, and Italians. For the first time, many voluntary immigrants were not Christians; Jews, particularly from eastern Europe, began arriving in large numbers. Industrialized Britain and Germany were prospering and jobs there were plentiful. But there was little industry in eastern and southern Europe. Life was harsh for poor land-hungry peasants. Also, some people—East European Jews, for example—were persecuted for their race and religion. Others left their homeland to escape political oppression. Polish men and women fled the hard rule of their Russian rulers.

Not only were immigrants anxious to escape the Old World, they were also drawn to the New. Relatives wrote to their families in Europe about the jobs to be found and the money to be made. Some immigrants actually believed the streets in the United States were paved with gold. Immigrants were attracted to America's democratic form of government and hoped for a warm welcome when they arrived. They were often disappointed. Many immigrants faced hostility from the nativists. These individuals claimed that the newcomers' languages, customs, and ideas upset the American way of life.

Some of this was old-fashioned prejudice. Some was resentment that unskilled men worked for lower pay and took the jobs of native-born Americans. And some was a fear that the left-wing ideas common in the immigrants' homelands were a threat to democracy and free enterprise.

School was a crucial experience for immigrant children. At home they spoke the language of the old country; at school they learned to speak English. At home, they absorbed their parents' culture; at school, they learned American customs and values.

Immigrants crossed the Atlantic in steerage—in the cramped, dirty, windowless, cargo areas of ships reserved for the poorest passengers. At New York's Castle Garden or Ellis Island they were inspected for disease. Those who arrived sick or without useful job skills were sent back to Europe. Names were often changed for the convenience of the officials who interviewed them. Families traveled together, or men came alone and brought the rest of the family over when they had jobs.

1 What is the author's main purpose in writing the essay?

A to show that most immigrants grew wealthy in America

B to show the role that immigration played in U.S. history

C to outline the requirements of immigrating to the U.S.

D to explain how schools dealt with immigrant children

2 Which was the LEAST important reason people came to the U.S.?

F to explore new ways of writing, painting, and composing music

G because they were slaves or indentured servants

H to escape persecution

J because of famine in their native land

3 Study the chart. Which group came to America at the end of the 19th and early in the 20th centuries?

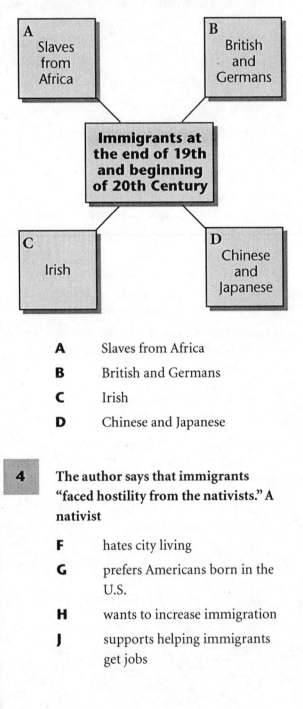

A Slaves from Africa

B British and Germans

C Irish

D Chinese and Japanese

4 The author says that immigrants "faced hostility from the nativists." A nativist

F hates city living

G prefers Americans born in the U.S.

H wants to increase immigration

J supports helping immigrants get jobs

5 Which taught immigrant children most about American culture?

   A   work

   B   church

   C   movies

   D   school

6 Why were immigrants needed in America?

   F   as workers

   G   as artists

   H   as politicians

   J   as teachers

7 The article says that immigrants crossed the Atlantic in "cramped, dirty, windowless cargo areas of the ship." Why did they do this?

   A   There wasn't any room on the rest of the ship.

   B   The immigrants liked to be together.

   C   The immigrants were afraid of looking out of the windows at the ocean.

   D   The immigrants didn't have much money.

8 Why did immigrants stop at Ellis Island?

   F   They were required by law.

   G   They wanted to visit the island.

   H   Their relatives were staying there.

   J   They were given money and food there.

Go On

Directions

This is the story about a wealthy man and a poor tailor. Read "Not Even for Gold." Then do Numbers 9 through 16.

Not Even for Gold

A WEALTHY OLD MAN lived in a grand house next door to a poor tailor and his wife. The tailor sang to himself as he went about his work. From morning to night, the wealthy man heard his neighbor singing.

The tailor enjoyed singing. It seemed to make his work go faster, and it drove away all his cares. When he sang, the tailor did not worry about how much he had earned that week. He did not worry about how many bills he had left to pay. He did not think of anything except his singing and his work.

In the early afternoon, the wealthy old man would take a nap. At the same time, the tailor would be working—and singing. Whenever the tailor hit a high note, his neighbor woke up. The old man was very upset at being jolted out of his sleep. It made him feel terrible for the rest of the day. Day after day, the tailor woke up the wealthy old man, and the wealthy old man felt worse and worse.

At last, the old man could stand it no longer. He went to knock at the tailor's door. "My sleep is worth a great deal to me," the rich man told his neighbor. "I'll give you eight pieces of gold a day if you'll stop singing."

"What a great piece of luck!" the tailor thought. "Now I'll be able to pay my bills!"

The next day the tailor worked, but this time he did not sing. The wealthy old man slept as soundly as a baby. When he woke up, he felt better than he had in years.

"A good nap is well worth the price I'm paying," he thought with a smile.

But the tailor was not smiling. Now that he could not sing, he began to worry about all sorts of things. Also, the joy vanished from his work. His needle dragged as he worked. By the end of one day without singing, the tailor felt worse than he ever had in his life.

The tailor went to the wealthy man's house. "I know that you need your sleep," he said. "But I need my song to be happy. I must go on singing. But I have a plan. While you're napping, I'll just hum softly. That way, you'll have your sleep, and I'll have my song." Then he handed the gold back to his neighbor. "I can't trade my song for anything in the world," the tailor said, "not even for gold!"

9 This story is mostly about

A a tailor who liked to sing

B a greedy man

C a rich person who didn't like tailors

D a clever tailor

10 The tailor said that the gold was "a piece of luck." What did he mean?

F One of the gold pieces was lucky.

G He would be able to pay his bills.

H He thought his singing was worth the money.

J He wanted to be like the rich man.

11 Why did the wealthy man offer the tailor gold?

A so the tailor would make him a suit

B so the tailor would have enough to eat

C so the tailor could have a vacation

D so the tailor would stop singing

12 The tailor gave the gold back to the wealthy man because

F he thought he was given too many gold pieces

G he wanted to sing while he worked

H he couldn't sew anymore

J he wanted to have the wealthy man's house

13 Why did the wealthy man say that "a good nap is well worth the price I'm paying"?

A He thought that sleeping was better than sewing.

B He wanted the tailor to stop sewing.

C He was very generous.

D He finally had some rest.

14 When the tailor sang he

F bothered his wife

G was off key

H didn't sew very well

J didn't worry

15 At the end, the tailor was shown as

A angry

B dishonest

C generous

D wise

16 If the wealthy man said he would give the tailor 20 gold coins if he would stop humming, the tailor would probably

F tell the rich man he wanted more gold coins

G refuse the gold and continue to hum

H take the gold and put it in the bank

J give the gold to his wife so she could buy a new outfit

Go On

Directions

This passage is part of the speech made by former First Lady Barbara Bush at a commencement at Wellesley College in Massachusetts in June, 1990. Wellesley is an all-female college. Although her comments are specifically for the women of the graduating class, they relate to all people, male and female.

…Wellesley, you see, is not just a place … but an idea … an experiment in excellence in which diversity is not just tolerated, but is embraced.

The essence of this spirit was captured in a moving speech about tolerance given last year by the student body President of one of your sister colleges. She related the story by Robert Fulghum[1] about a young pastor who, finding himself in charge of some very energetic children, hit upon a game called "Giants, Wizards and Dwarfs." "You have to decide now," the pastor instructed the children, "which you are … a giant, a wizard or a dwarf?" At that, a small girl tugging on his pants leg, asked, "But where do the mermaids stand?."

The pastor told her there are no mermaids. "Oh yes there are," she said. "I am a mermaid."

This little girl knew what she was and she was not about to give up on either her identity or the game. She intended to take her place wherever mermaids fit into the scheme of things. Where do the mermaids stand … all those who are different, those who do not fit the boxes and the pigeonholes? "Answer that question," wrote Fulghum, "and you can build a school, a nation, or a whole world on it."

As that very wise young woman said … "diversity … like anything worth having … requires effort." Effort to learn about and respect difference, to be compassionate with one another, to cherish our own identity … and to accept unconditionally the same in all others.

You should all be very proud that this is the Wellesley spirit. Now I know your first choice for today was Alice Walker[2], known for The Color Purple. Instead you got me—known for … the color of my hair! Of course, Alice Walker's book has a special resonance here. At Wellesley, each class is known by a special color … and for four years the Class of '90 has worn the color purple. Today you meet on Severance Green to say goodbye to all that … to begin a new and very personal journey … a search for your own true colors.

In the world that awaits you beyond the shores of Lake Waban, no one can say what your true colors will be. But this I know: You have a first class education from a first class school. And so you need not, probably cannot, live a "paint-by numbers" life. Decisions are not irrevocable. Choices do come back.

As you set off from Wellesley, I hope that many of you will consider making three very special choices.

The first is to believe in something larger than yourself … to get involved in some of the big ideas of your time. I chose literacy because I honestly believe that if more people could read, write and comprehend, we would be that much closer to solving so many of the problems plaguing our society.

---

[1] Robert Fulghum is a writer and former minister.
[2] Alice Walker is an African American novelist.

Early on I made another choice which I hope you will make as well. Whether you are talking about education, career or service, you are talking about life . . . and life must have joy. It's supposed to be fun.

One of the reasons I made the most important decision of my life . . . to marry George Bush . . . is because he made me laugh. It's true, sometimes we've laughed through our tears . . . but that shared laughter has been one of our strongest bonds. Find the joy in life, because as Ferris Bueller[3] said on his day off . . . "Life moves pretty fast. Ya don't stop and look around once in a while, ya gonna miss it!"

The third choice that must not be missed is to cherish your human connections: your relationships with friends and family. For several years, you've had impressed upon you the importance to your career of dedication and hard work. This is true, but as important as your obligations as a doctor, lawyer or business leader will be, you are a human being first and those human connections—with spouses, with children, with friends—are the most important investments you will ever make.

At the end of your life, you will never regret not having passed one more test, not winning one more verdict or not closing one more deal. You will regret time not spent with a husband, a friend, a child or a parent.

We are in a transitional period right now . . . fascinating and exhilarating times . . . learning to adjust to the changes and the choices we . . . men and women . . . are facing. I remember what a friend said, on hearing her husband lament to his buddies that he had to babysit. Quickly setting him straight my friend told her husband that "when it's your own kids it's not called babysitting!"

Maybe we should adjust faster, maybe slower, but whatever the era . . . whatever the times, one thing will never change: fathers and mothers, if you have children they must come first. Your success as a family . . . our success as a society depends not on what happens at the White House, but on what happens inside your house.

---

[3] *Ferris Bueller's Day Off* was a popular 1980's movie about a teenage guy, played by Matthew Broderick, who takes a day off from school.

17 What advice does Mrs. Bush give in this speech?

    A   Put work first.

    B   Put family first.

    C   Put school first.

    D   Don't try to be different.

18 Which statement from the speech shows the important part of Mrs. Bush's advice?

    F   "We are in a transitional period right now…"

    G   "You have a first class education from a first class school."

    H   "You will regret time not spent with a husband, a friend, a child or a parent."

    J   "For several years, you've had impressed upon you the importance to your career of dedication and hard work."

19 What virtue is LEAST emphasized in Mrs. Bush's talk?

    A   the importance of obeying your parents

    B   the importance of following your own path

    C   the importance of a good education

    D   the importance of joy and happiness

20 In the story told by Robert Fulghum, the mermaid stands for

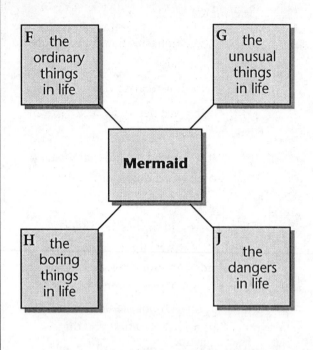

    F   the ordinary things in life

    G   the unusual things in life

    H   the boring things in life

    J   the dangers in life

21 Mrs. Bush said you "needn't live a 'paint-by-numbers' life." What does she mean?

    A   living by following rules others have given you

    B   living a life filled with compassion and caring for others

    C   living a life which is different from most others

    D   living a life where you make careful decisions about what you want to do and be

22 What is the most likely reason that Mrs. Bush told the story about the mermaid?

F to emphasize the importance of diversity

G to show that she is well-read

H to warn her audience of trouble ahead

J to remind people that life with no education is difficult

23 Mrs. Bush said that Alice Walker's book "has a special resonance here." What does *resonance* mean as used here?

A desire

B work

C fear

D meaning

24 Mrs. Bush said she believes strongly in the importance of knowing how to read and write. What reason does she NOT give for literacy's importance?

F Literacy creates communication.

G Literacy creates understanding.

H Literacy can solve social problems.

J Literacy is critical for military work.

Go On

NOTICE: Photocopying any part of this book is forbidden by law.

141

Directions

In this part of the test, you will listen to two passages. One is written by a person who moved to New York City from Puerto Rico in the 1970's. The other is by a person who moved from Italy to the U.S. in 1911. Then you will answer some questions to show how well you understood what was read.

You will listen to the passages twice. The first time you hear the essays, listen carefully but do not take notes. As you listen to the essays the second time, you may take notes. You may use these notes to answer the questions that follow. Use the space below for your notes.

NOTES

STOP

NOTICE: Photocopying any part of this book is forbidden by law.

143

Using specific details from the passage, complete the chart below by giving the reasons that Eddie Miranda's and Theresa Avena's families moved to New York City.

Eddie Miranda' s Family	Theresa Avena's Family

26 How was life different in New York City from Puerto Rico for Eddie Miranda? Use information from the essay to support your answer.

_____

_____

_____

_____

_____

_____

27 Theresa Avena wanted to go home soon after she arrived because she had a lot of difficulties. What were these difficulties? Do you think other newcomers to New York from Europe, Asia, or other places also had a hard time at first? Use details form the essay to support your answer.

_____

_____

_____

_____

_____

_____

Go On

Planning Page

Use this page to plan your answer for Number 28, but do not write your final answer here. Write your final answer beginning on the next page.

28   Discuss the feelings of both Eddie Miranda and Theresa Avena about their new homes.

In your discussion, be sure to include

- descriptions of difficulties they may have faced
- a comparison of their attitudes toward their new homes
- how each person is affected by the move to a new land

Check your writing for correct spelling grammar, and punctuation.

_____

_____

_____

_____

_____

_____

_____

_____

_____

_____

_____

_____

_____

_____

_____

_____

_____

_____

_____

_____

STOP

Session 2

Directions

You will read an article called "The Door of No Return" and a poem called "Liberty and Slavery." The article is about an island that was very important in the history of slavery. The poem is written by a man who was born into slavery in the United States and became free.

First you will answer questions and write about what you have read. You may look back at the article and the poem as often as you like. Then you will be asked to write an essay.

Now turn the page and begin.

African Americans knew that once they came to this island they would never return to their homes.

The Door of No Return

A small island off the coast of Senegal in western Africa has been aptly termed the closest approximation to hell we will ever see on earth. Goreé Island was the place where captured Africans were sent to be chained, branded, sold, and then loaded onto crowded slave ships to be transported like cattle to work in the fields of the New World during the 17th and 18th centuries.

Husbands, wives, and children were separated with callous indifference to the effect on their lives. Cruel overseers collected groups of six men and women and bound them together with neck irons, leg chains, and heavy weights. Those who attempted to resist were first beaten and then, if there were any further attempts to resist, there were slowly and painfully hanged to serve as a terrible example to others.

Many of the slaves were kept in a round stone fortress which is now the Goreé Historical Museum. Locally it is still referred to as "the prison." Today its once dark and dismal rooms are filled with exhibits displaying the realities of the slave trade and the terrible events that happened there.

Goreé Island was engaged in that barbarous trade for over 200 years. This hellish island destroyed the lives of hundreds of thousands of people. Today, the slave rooms continue to enact the same painful scenes on a daily basis, but now those playing the parts of slaves are actors and the onlookers are not plantation owners but hundreds of tourists every day. The visitors' attitude is quite different now than before. The commercial indifference to suffering which was

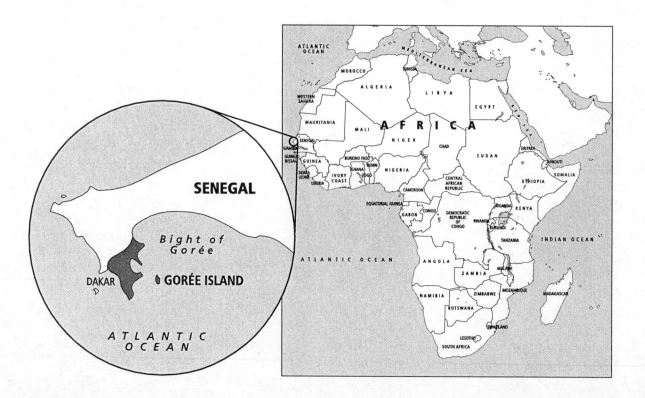

typical of that time in history has been replaced with a conscious horror at the inhumanity of people to others.

The most painful and soul-wrenching sight of all is the "door of no return," which is located in a building known as the Maison des Esclaves (House of Slaves). The building was home to a French merchant who lived on Goreé Island and sold slaves to the captains of European ships enroute to America. The merchant lived in the upper floors of the house and downstairs, where the slaves were imprisoned until they were sold, is a doorway which looks out on the open sea. It is known as "the door of no return" because slaves who passed through that door were loaded onto slave ships and separated from Africa forever, brutally torn from their former home and family.

Visitors include such famous statesmen as the Pope, the President of the United States, Nelson Mandela, and world leaders from everywhere, as well as ordinary people from all over the world, particularly African Americans from the United States. They are joined in their shared compassion for the foul deeds that occurred in the name of what was then considered "business."

The slave trade is over but the memory of that evil remains.

29 Complete the chart with words or phrases that describe the slave traders. Identify information from the article that supports each character trait.

Character Trait	Supporting Information

 30 How does the author feel about slavery? Explain your answer using details from the article.

_____

_____

_____

_____

_____

_____

Go On

Liberty and Slavery

By George Moses Horton

Alas! And am I born for this,
To wear this slavish chain?
Deprived of all created bliss,
Through hardship, toil and pain!

How long have I in bondage lain,
And longed to be free!
Alas! And must I still complain—
Deprived of liberty.

Oh, Heaven and is there no relief
This side the silent grave—
To sooth the pain—to stop the grief
And anguish of a slave?

Come Liberty, thou cheerful sound,
Roll through my ravished ear!
Come, let my grief in joys be drowned,
And drive away my fears.

31　What is most likely the poet's purpose in writing this poem? Use ideas from the poem to support your answer.

_____

_____

_____

_____

_____

_____

Go On

Planning Page

You may PLAN your writing for Number 32 here if you wish, but do NOT write your final answer on this page. Your writing on this Planning Page will NOT count toward your final score. Write your final answer beginning on the next page.

32 Choose a line or lines from this poem. Discuss the meaning of your selection, and explain how it applies to the selection on Goreé Island. Use ideas from BOTH the poem and the article in your answer.

In your answer, be sure to include

- The line or lines you have selected from the poem
- An explanation of how your selection applies to the article on Gore Island

Check your writing for correct spelling, grammar, and punctuation.

_____

_____

_____

_____

_____

_____

_____

_____

_____

_____

_____

_____

_____

_____

Go On

33 Write an essay about a person in history or someone you know who has overcome obstacles to attain what he or she wanted.

In your article, be sure to include

- who the person is
- what he or she did
- the challenges he or she faced
- how the challenges were overcome
- an introduction, a body, and a conclusion

_____

_____

_____

_____

_____

_____

_____

_____

_____

_____

_____

_____

_____

_____

_____

_____

_____

NOTICE: Photocopying any part of this book is forbidden by law.

159

STOP